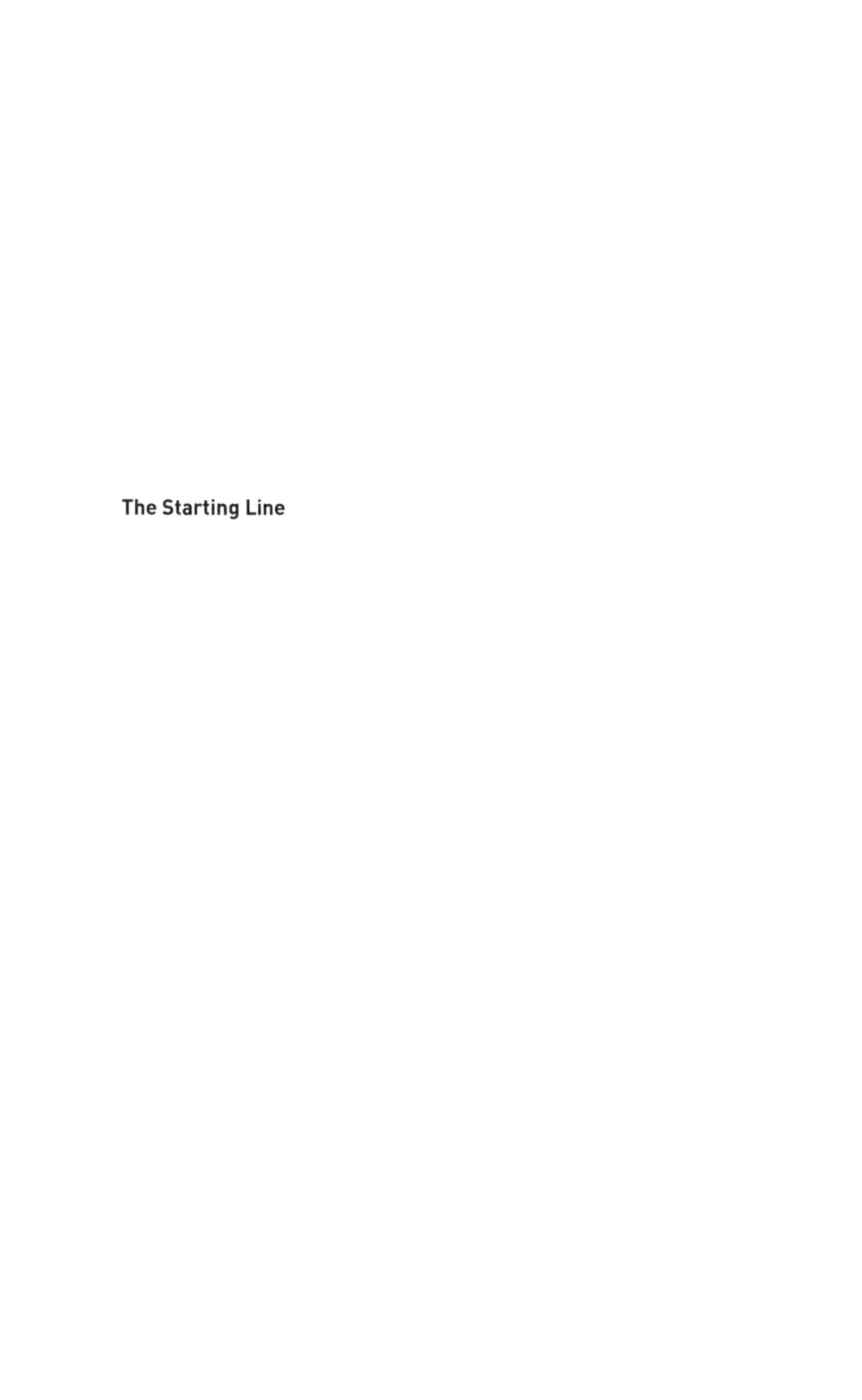

The Starting Line

The Starting Line

Latina/o Children, Texas Schools, and National Debates on Early Education

ROBERT CROSNOE
WITH CLAUDE BONAZZO AND AIDA RAMOS

University of Texas Press   *Austin*

Copyright © 2020 by the University of Texas Press
All rights reserved
Printed in the United States of America
First edition, 2020

Requests for permission to reproduce material from this work should be sent to:
   Permissions
   University of Texas Press
   P.O. Box 7819
   Austin, TX 78713-7819
   utpress.utexas.edu/rp-form

All images are courtesy of the author

♾ The paper used in this book meets the minimum requirements of ANSI/NISO Z39.48-1992 (R1997) (Permanence of Paper).

Library of Congress Cataloging-in-Publication Data
Names: Crosnoe, Robert, author.
Title: The starting line : Latina/o children, Texas schools, and national debates on early education / Robert Crosnoe ; with Claude Bonazzo and Aida Ramos.
Description: First edition. | Austin : University of Texas Press, 2020. | Includes bibliographical references and index.
Identifiers: LCCN 2020027884
ISBN 978-1-4773-2238-3 (cloth)
ISBN 978-1-4773-2239-0 (library ebook)
ISBN 978-1-4773-2240-6 (ebook)
Subjects: LCSH: Hispanic American children—Education (Preschool)—Texas. | Low-income students—Education (Preschool)—Texas. | Hispanic American children—Education (Preschool)—United States—Case studies. | Hispanic American children—Education (Preschool)—Texas—Evaluation. | Educational change—United States.
Classification: LCC LC2670.2 .C76 2020 | DDC 371.829/68073—dc23
LC record available at https://lccn.loc.gov/2020027884

doi:10.7560/322383

*For my own students and everyone's students.
For my own children and everyone's children.*

Contents

Preface **ix**

Acknowledgments **xiii**

Introduction: National Issues through a Local Lens   1

1. The Importance of Connections in Early Childhood Education   **27**
2. Connecting Classrooms to Classrooms   **40**
3. Connecting Families, Schools, and Communities   **62**
4. Connecting Academic and Socioemotional Goals   **88**
5. Connecting Needs and Challenges   **111**

Conclusion: The Big Picture   **133**

Works Cited   **154**

Index   **165**

Preface

I have spent a great deal of time in different kinds of schools, and they all have their own kind of magic. Throughout most of my career, I have been interested in what high schools are like, and whenever I am in a high school, I am deeply struck by the way hordes of teenagers flow through classrooms and hallways. It is a magic of energy and rhythm. In the 2000s, my focus shifted to little kids, partly because my own children were young at that time but also because early childhood education was facing increasing attention from policy makers. Unlike the larger and more diverse high schools I have studied, the many preschool classrooms I have visited and observed typically serve a more homogeneous student population of young, low-income Latina/o children, many or most of whom come in as English language learners. The magic of these classrooms is more about a kind of mayhem; they are filled with noise, movement, laughter, and hugs, and more than anything else, they just seem alive. I leave them a bit overwhelmed, suffering from sensory overload, but also excited and hopeful.

Amid this magical mayhem, something else becomes clear upon reflection when I am back in the quiet of my office or home. Underlying all of it is a calm and steady ethos of caring, with teachers who are invested in the children they are serving, children who are engaged in their learning, parents who are dedicated to both, and an order the caring gives to the seeming chaos that makes clear the educational goals at work. Within this ethos of caring, people seem dedicated to the idea that early childhood education matters, that there will be rewards if they get it right and consequences if they do not. They care. Consequently, most of the teachers seem to be on the lookout for how to make things work better. They seem to believe in what they are doing but also believe that there is room for improvement.

As a researcher studying early childhood education, I have taken a cue from these educators and the families they serve by believing in the system and what it represents while also searching for how it might get better. This book is my attempt to do so in ways that recognize strengths, identify opportunities to get stronger, and harness the incredible zeal for change on the ground. It is based on my years as a researcher involved in national discussions of early childhood education to promote policies that enhance the future prospects of vulnerable groups of children. It is also based on my years of conducting extensive research within early childhood education programs in my home state of Texas, serving a particularly vulnerable group with great potential to respond to such policy investments.

Through these experiences I have developed an argument about early childhood education and its role in the future of the growing Latina/o population in Texas and the United States as a whole. The argument has three basic principles:

- Increasing the number of young children from historically disadvantaged segments of society in high-quality early childhood education is a potentially effective strategy for combatting persistent inequalities in educational attainment, including those related to the large, growing, and often threatened Latina/o population.
- This goal can be supported by a holistic approach recognizing the different ways that early childhood education classrooms are connected to the larger contexts in which they are situated and encompass a complex exchange of academic and social processes.
- Such an approach requires careful attention to the daily experiences of children, their teachers, and their parents in and around early childhood education classrooms, and the Texas public prekindergarten (pre-K) program is an ideal place to do just that for Latina/o children.

In this book, with some help from two of my former students, I will take a deep dive into each of the three points of this argument. Doing so involves laying out the national debates about early childhood education and Latina/o children, using Texas as a case for learning about and from these debates, then moving them forward, and going into classrooms in a large, heavily Latina/o, urban district in Texas to give a glimpse of what is going on and hear the human voices involved.

Motivating this activity is a simple pair of questions: What about early childhood education for Latina/o children is working, and what needs to be improved? Answering these driving questions is my goal in this book. This goal is important because the stakes are indeed high, right now and for the future. They are high for the individual children from diverse backgrounds who increasingly will need educational success to thrive in their lives. They are high for a society in and out of Texas that increasingly depends on having an educated populace and workforce but still is divided by racial/ethnic, socioeconomic, and other kinds of inequalities that undermine that mission. These educational stakes play out over children's academic careers, which last many years and cross many institutions. If one thinks of education as a journey, early childhood education is the starting line. Getting things right at this starting line may solve a lot of problems on the journey. That is why the world is watching.

I had my own journey to the discovery of the importance of the starting line, which grew out of the aforementioned gradual shift in my research interests from secondary school and adolescence to early childhood and early education. In retrospect, there were four important factors underlying this journey, most but not all professional. The first was that in 2004 I was asked to join the Eunice Kennedy Shriver National Institute of Child Health and Human Development (NICHD) Early Child Care Research Network, which was a collection of researchers running a national study funded by the National Institutes of Health to determine the effects of early child care on child development (NICHD Early Child Care Research Network, 2005). In that network, I was surrounded by top early childhood education scholars, and they had a huge influence on me. In particular, they showed me how what I was studying among adolescents in high school could not be separated from what happened to those adolescents when they were young.

The second was that around the same time, there was a great deal of public discussion about findings reported from long-term follow-ups of pioneering early childhood education programs primarily serving low-income African American and white children. Led by such luminaries as Nobel Prize–winning economist James Heckman, these studies drew on experimental designs to isolate the effects of participation in these programs early in life on adult outcomes decades later. They demonstrated that such programs did have long-term effects. More importantly, they also demonstrated that education-focused early childhood interventions brought greater long-term returns on investment than did programs targeting older children, adolescents, and young adults (Heckman, 2006).

The third factor in my shift toward early childhood education research was that from 2003 to 2006, I was part of a "young scholars" program supported by the Foundation for Child Development. The goal of this program was to encourage scholars studying immigration to focus on the early childhood years. I had long been involved in research on the education and health of immigrant youth. I was open to the idea of studying young children, although I have to admit that at the time, I was skeptical that I would find anything among little kids that would interest me more than what teenagers were doing. This program opened me up to a new way of thinking about immigration and the introduction of immigrant families to US institutions (Crosnoe, 2006). Presenting research from that project gave me the opportunity to hear from Latina/o communities about my own blind spots, including a tendency to discuss inequality in terms of deficits rather than shifting conversation to the possibility of using strengths to reduce inequality. I was very defensive at first, but I learned a great deal once I got over that defensiveness and listened. I am still learning.

The fourth factor was far more personal. Around the time that these other events were going on (2004–2006), I became a father not once but twice. That transition ushered me into a new era of my life in which I spent a lot of time in early child care programs and preschools and spent even more time thinking about what was best for my children then and in the future. That period was the first time in which I saw my research self and my private-life self converge.

Through these experiences, I came to see early childhood education as a critical component of the educational system and of the life course, and my research followed this growing recognition. I learned so much in the process, including that I could not simply convert how I did things and how I thought about things from one stage/period to another. For the most part, however, what was missing from these experiences was an explicit consideration of the special needs, strengths, and challenges of young Latina/o children and their families. I lived in a state at the demographic forefront of the country, so I knew that Latina/o education was increasingly the agenda-setter for US education. I also knew from years of conducting immigration research that the Latina/o population was not just growing but diversifying in ways that had to be taken into account. Yet, I often found myself wondering why Latina/o children and their families were not in the center frame of the research and policy discussion more often and more consistently. Attention to them, tailoring the understanding of early childhood education to their unique experiences, and enriching theory through this deeper understanding are pressing needs.

Fortunately, there have been many other scholars who have recognized those needs and pushed the field to better address them; I cite many of those scholars throughout this book. I joined their cause. I think that I can speak for many of them as I open this book by writing that although we all know a lot about early childhood education for Latina/o children, we still have a lot to learn about this issue, and we must keep pushing.

Acknowledgments

Direct support for the research described in this book came from the Foundation for Child Development (FCD), supplemented by the National Institute of Child Health and Human Development and the Institute of Education Sciences. For many years, FCD has played a major role in pushing the issue of early childhood education for Latina/o children, especially those from immigrant families, into the spotlight. Its support has had immeasurable impact on my own work, and I could not be more appreciative. In particular, I owe a debt of gratitude to the former FCD president Ruby Takanishi, who has guided me in so many ways.

I also received a great deal of direct support from the research and evaluation office of the pseudonymous Southwest Independent School District, the principals and vice principals of the nine SWISD schools that participated in this research, the nearly five dozen SWISD teachers who let us into their classrooms and talked with us at length, and the more than two dozen SWISD parents who took time out of their hectic schedules of raising young children to sit down with us to discuss their children's schools. SWISD is a good school district with much to admire, and I am glad that it is doing what it does.

At the University of Texas, I received incredible support from the staff of the Population Research Center, particularly Mary De La Garza, Sylvia Celedon, and Meghan Thomson; the Department of Sociology, especially Julie Kniseley; and the College of Liberal Arts, especially Erica Whittington, as I tried to keep an extensive research program afloat while taking on new responsibilities. There are also my many colleagues at the PRC and in the Department of Sociology and College of Liberal Arts who have a hand in almost anything I do.

For this project I owe a pronounced level of gratitude to my students who participated in the SWISD research with gusto, among them Jessica Dunning-Lozano, Anna Thornton, Claude Bonazzo, and Aida Ramos, as well as Dani Rosales. Claude and Aida went beyond carrying a heavy load in data collection. They also helped me on some of the early writings from the project that made their way into this book in various forms. That is why they more than deserve to have their names associated with this book alongside mine.

Lastly, I always have to thank my kids, Joseph and Caroline, whose early childhood education experiences helped get me into this topic, and their mother, Shannon, for being next to me on that ride.

The Starting Line

INTRODUCTION

National Issues through a Local Lens

The context for asking and answering the driving questions of this book is the broad national level. A good understanding of what is going on at that level can lead to understanding specific classrooms in a specific city in a specific state. Coming full circle, efforts to shed light on what is happening on the local level can then guide debates and decision-making back up at the national level. There are national trends converging to draw attention to the early childhood education of young Latina/o children in the United States, and those trends are crystallized in the state of Texas. I designed, and my team of graduate students and I conducted, a study in Texas as a local entree into that national discussion.

Three National Trends of Interest

In that spirit, the three national trends motivating this book require careful examination. Two of them concern shifts in educational policy and practice, and one concerns a major national-level population change. All three of these trends are on clear display in Texas.

The Push for Early Childhood Education

Early childhood education has become a focal point of educational policy and practice, drawing more attention and investment and serving a much broader swath of the child population of the United States. What is behind this trend?

Although early childhood education comes in many forms, it can be thought of in the most general terms as preschool programs for young children with the goal of preparing them for elementary school through the provision of structured curricula. The guiding philosophy is that early childhood is a critical time in the development of children's academic and cognitive skills that then serve as a foundation on which all subsequent learning and achievement are based. Consequently, children with some exposure to early childhood education will be better positioned to do well once they are in school (Crosnoe et al., 2015). This philosophy is evidence-based, at least in part.

The number of children in early childhood education programs began steadily rising over the last decades of the twentieth century, reflecting the growing awareness of the promise of educational value for children but also the acute need for early child care linked to rising maternal employment and the political push for early child care associated with the women's rights movement (Clark-Stewart & Allhusen, 2005). For many years, however, early childhood education tended to primarily serve the children of more socioeconomically advantaged and usually white parents who used their financial and other resources to purchase early child care for their children that also provided educational opportunities for those children to get ahead. Along with many other factors, the differential exposure to early childhood education was a reason that children from low-income and especially low-income racial/ethnic minority populations tended to start formal schooling at an academic disadvantage compared to their more affluent and, often, white peers. They had less formally structured opportunity for skill development while young and entered school poised to be compared unfavorably to their peers. Given the highly cumulative nature of the US educational system, in which everything builds on what came before, each step setting the stage for the next, such an initial disadvantage can then grow over time. This process widens disparities between children and among groups of children over time to create the well-documented and problematic gaps in educational attainment by socioeconomic status and race/ethnicity that are widely viewed as a failure of the system (Alexander et al., 2014; Lee & Burkham, 2002; Waldfogel, 2006; Zigler et al., 2006).

As awareness has grown of the role of differential exposure to early childhood education in long-term educational inequality, so too has recognition that expanding access to early childhood education might be an effective policy tool for reducing educational inequality. That expansion has largely been a public enterprise. Most Americans are familiar with Head Start, which is the federal early childhood education program started in the 1960s to serve four-year-old children of low-income and predominantly racial/ethnic minority families. In the ensuing decades, Head Start expanded the services it provides for academic enrichment as well as the eligible age range to include many three-year-olds and the population it targets to a growing share of Head Start children from immigrant backgrounds (Duncan & Magnuson, 2013; Ludwig & Phillips, 2007; Puma et al., 2010).

More recently, most states have created their own publicly subsidized preschool programs. Some (often blue states) have been motivated by concerns about equity, while others (often red states) have been motivated by hopes for future economic impact. Like Head Start, most of these state-sponsored programs have special eligibility criteria limiting enrollment to children from more disadvantaged backgrounds or who have special educational needs, such as English language learners. In many cases, early childhood education is conducted at public elementary schools; such programs are often labeled "pre-K" (Bogard & Takanishi, 2005; Duncan & Magnuson, 2013; Fuller, 2007; Gormley et al., 2005). This trend then reverberates back to the federal level. In 2013, President Barack Obama's early childhood education initiative devoted substantial resources to federal-state partnerships to expand public pre-K programs as well as Head Start and other federal early childhood programs (White House, 2013). Some of that investment was rolled back in 2017 by the Trump administration (Loewenberg et al., 2017).

As a result of these federal and state initiatives, early childhood education enrollment has risen and become less discrepant across diverse groups, although enrollment is far from universal or evenly distributed across the population. This progress has been backed up by a wealth of correlational evidence linking attendance in early childhood education programs with higher levels of academic skills upon school entry and then academic achievement during school. Notably, the benefits tend to be larger for children from low-income and racial/ethnic populations, including low-income Latina/o Americans. The evidence base does have critics who have argued that such correlations might not reflect cause and effect. Instead, the children who attend early childhood education might differ from children who do not in ways that then lead to more positive academic outcomes regardless of that attendance, such as more involved parents and more community resources. Experimental designs, which are the best method for establishing cause and effect, have allayed some of those concerns but reveal more moderate effects (Duncan & Magnuson, 2013; Gormley et al., 2005).

Thus, the contemporary expansion of early childhood education reflects a coherent philosophy and is built upon empirical evidence. In this light, there does not seem to be much room for debate. Yet, debate does continue. One reason concerns questions about the degree to which the moderate academic benefits of early childhood education for young children starting school warrant the price tag of such programs. Another concerns a "fade out" pattern that has emerged from evaluations of Head Start, state pre-K, and other early childhood education programs. Fading out means the differences in test scores between children who did and did not attend early childhood education steadily decrease and even disappear as they move through elementary school; the pattern seems to defy the argument that the cumulative nature of educational systems determines that what happens at the starting line sets the whole course of a person's education (Bailey et al., 2017; Brooks-Gunn, 2003; Ludwig & Phillips, 2007). A complicating factor is that decades-long experimental evaluations of some pioneering early childhood education programs have revealed that fade-out in academic and cognitive skills associated with program enrollment is eventually followed by other kinds of benefits in adulthood, including greater educational attainment and less involvement with the criminal justice system. Notably, these adult benefits mean that the original dollar investments in the early childhood education programs were paid back many times over across multiple decades (Barnett & Masse, 2007; Heckman, 2006; Schweinhart et al., 2005).

The bottom line, then, is that early childhood education helps children from more disadvantaged families and communities start school with greater academic preparation, does not help them out-learn or out-achieve other children over time, but does help them become more productive and stable adults. In this way, returns on investment are sufficient to justify the expansion of early childhood education, but that does not mean the contemporary system of early childhood education is without substantial room for improvement. One facet would be what kinds of rewards might emerge if fade-out diminished. The growing PK-3 movement, to promote the view of the critical period of early learning as pre-K through third grade, is based on an argument that the key is to consider early childhood education not as a "pre" stage of the educational system, as the before in the before/after transition from early childhood into school, but instead as part of single educational process linking and coordinating instruction and learning from preschool through the primary grades. PK-3 advocates recommend stepping back to consider a multiyear sequence of educational experiences that will shed light on where fade-out happens as a means of promoting sustainability of preschool gains (Bogard & Takanishi, 2005).

Answering the driving questions of this book—*What about early childhood education for Latina/o children is working, and what needs to be improved?*—will do just that, wading into the national debate about who is and is not benefiting from the expansion of early childhood education (and why and why not).

The Emphasis on Standards and Accountability

The expansion of early educational opportunities for young children has converged with the growing public and private emphasis on academic standards and accountability in educational settings. The convergence has shifted the way that early childhood education is organized and evaluated. What are the reasons behind and implications of this shift?

The standards and accountability movement of recent decades began in relation to the public kindergarten through 12th grade (K-12) system. Basically, its proponents contend that public elementary, middle, and high schools should be evaluated and funded according to hard evidence about how well they are doing their jobs according to fixed standards. A big part of this movement is that schools that are not doing a good job should be held accountable. In general, criteria have been based on standardized test scores, with schools tasked with improving students' overall test score performance over time and reducing socioeconomic, racial/ethnic, language-based, and other kinds of disparities in such performance. Once set, the performance benchmarks then drive curricular and pedagogical decisions, with the goal established first, followed by the development of strategies to meet the goal. How schools are doing vis-à-vis their performance benchmarks is made public, and the resulting accountability takes the form of improvement plans and, eventually, low-performing schools' reorganization and/or closure. This movement is perhaps best embodied by and publicly identified with the federal No Child Left Behind legislation enacted by the George W. Bush administration in the early 2000s, largely inspired by the president's educational reforms in Texas while he was governor. This educational reform had many champions and many critics; despite being subsequently modified during the Obama administration, it has had an outsized influence on setting the agenda of educational policy and practice (Darling-Hammond, 2006; Gamoran, 2007).

In many ways, the standards and accountability movement is built on the idea that if the government is investing so much in education, it should know what it is getting in return. As government investment in early childhood education has grown, the trickling down of this idea into that sector of the educational system probably should not be that surprising, especially given that many state pre-K programs have been sold as ways of developing a more productive workforce. Many who are not steeped in the world of early childhood education find it sensible to transfer this increasingly dominant approach of elementary and secondary education to preschool learning as well. Doing so seems less sensible to those who are steeped in the influential perspective of early childhood education that explicitly views it as distinct from formal schooling, given how different young children are from older children and adolescents. That approach, often referred to as "developmentally appropriate practices," contends that the role of early child education is to foster the development of the whole child—cognitively, socially, emotionally, physically—as a means of preparing children for school and for life more generally. It involves designing programmatic activities that are a good match with where children are developmentally and culturally and a more expansive focus on what learning entails. Early childhood education, in this view, is child-driven, not content-driven (Adair, 2014; Genishi & Dyson, 2009; Graue, 2008; Ryan & Grieshaber, 2005).

The developmentally appropriate practices approach has been critiqued as placing too much emphasis on a developmental focus, on tailoring learning to where children are developmentally, relative to a cultural focus, on grounding learning in respect for the cultural histories and traditions of students. This critique suggests bias involved in assessing what children need without being critical of how such assessments are socially constructed (who gets to define what is appropriate); that bias is certainly relevant to the topic of the early childhood education of Latina/o children (Brown & Lan, 2015; National Association for the Education of Young Children, 2019; Ryan & Grieshaber, 2005). I wade into that critique in the chapters of this book. Here, though, I want to problematize something else, which is the common perception that there is a clear distinction between standards and accountability on one hand and developmentally appropriate practices on the other, that one is the academic agenda and the other is the nonacademic agenda with no connection between them. I and others see this seeming dichotomy as exaggerated.

For those endorsing that dichotomy, proponents of the standards and accountability movement think that the play-based nature of traditional early childhood education programs is "soft" and not sufficiently academic. They tend to latch onto fade-out evidence as backing up their argument. They do not think of academic activities as a core part of developmentally appropriate practices. Others who endorse that dichotomy but favor the developmentally appropriate practices side often argue that giving young children structured lessons with formal pedagogy and testing them is a real stretch and not how children learn or what children need. These proponents tend to stress evidence that early childhood education programs promote a range of adolescent and adult outcomes, even if not manifested in test scores. Yet, if academic learning can be supported in developmentally appropriate ways for young children, standards and accountability practices also may be adapted and refined for the early childhood education context (Fuller et al., 2017; Le et al., 2019; National Association for the Education of Young Children, 2019).

I do think the debate about standards and accountability versus developmentally appropriate practices has been useful in many ways. I also think the false dichotomy around this versus that has been created in public discussion limits the ability to find creative solutions to the special needs of vulnerable populations. So, perhaps I should put this false dichotomy aside and consider the goal of early childhood classrooms guided by developmentally appropriate practices implemented with more attention to accountability, integrating academic and developmental goals in service to each other.

The Changing Faces of America's Children

Much has been made of the "Latinization" of the United Sates, a term that refers to the rapid growth of the Latina/o population over the past several decades to become the second biggest racial/ethnic group in the country. It is on track to make up the largest share of US children in the not-so-distant future. This growing population has both needs and challenges, and the educational system often struggles to effectively serve them.

I will begin with the reasons for this rapid population change. The factor that garners the most attention is immigration from Latin American countries, especially Mexico. This immigration stream really took off after the passage of federal immigration reforms in 1965. This legislation lifted or eased many of the restrictions on immigration that had been in place for decades, including national origin quotas that had long favored European immigration and constrained how many Latin Americans settled in the United States. Afterward, immigration shifted quickly and dramatically to Latin America, which sent absolutely and relatively large numbers of immigrants into the United States for the next forty years, both through legal means and through undocumented entry. Another significant factor that receives less attention is the higher fertility rates of Latina/o Americans, particularly Latin American immigrants, relative to other large racial/ethnic groups in the United States. Indeed, in the twenty-first century, the greatest driving force of the growth of the Latina/o population in the United States is the larger number of children born in Latina/o immigrant families, not immigration itself (Flores, 2017; Tienda, 2009).

To some, this population change has been positive, for increasing the diversity of the nation, enriching its culture, and bolstering its pool of human resources. For others, it has been met with resistance and fear. The tension between these two forces reflects the challenges and strengths of this growing and, I need to stress, internally diverse group of Americans. In terms of challenges, Latina/o Americans are, on average, more socioeconomically disadvantaged than the general population, with families more likely to be in poverty, less likely to be headed by parents with high school diplomas and college degrees, and more likely to be headed by parents working in insecure sectors of the labor market such as service, manual labor, and agriculture. They also face a high level of ethnic- and immigration-based discrimination in the United States, especially Latina/o Americans with origins in Mexico and Central America, that has been tied to extreme political and legal hostility in recent years. Although framed around the issue of undocumented immigrants, such hostility affects many Latina/o Americans regardless of their immigrant origins or history in the United States. These socioeconomic, ethnic-based, and immigration-based challenges and threats are often combined with linguistic barriers. Specifically, Latina/o Americans with immigrant backgrounds often are still developing English skills, which can be a disadvantage in the US labor market and in other ways in a fraught climate in which being a Spanish speaker is itself a contested social identity (Flores, 2017; Hernandez, 2006; Markert, 2010).

Such challenges are then felt by Latina/o children, especially those from immigrant families, as they navigate the US educational system, which is socioeconomically stratified and ethnically segregated and does not have a good track record serving the needs of children from diverse linguistic backgrounds. Despite such clear family and community strengths as engaged parenting, strong social networks, and powerful work ethic that can bolster academic pursuits, Latina/o children facing social, economic, and institutional disadvantages may not reach their full academic potential. Indeed, Latina/o children in the United States have lower rates of school completion and educational attainment relative to the general population. As a result, they are often labeled "at risk" by the educational system. This label is one reason young Latina/o children are increasingly targeted for early childhood interventions including educational programs (Crosnoe et al., 2015; Fuller, 2007; Madrid, 2011; Mendez & Crosby, 2018; Reardon & Owens, 2014; Valdés, 1996).

This book takes as reality that Latina/o children and youth will disproportionately fill the halls and classrooms of US schools over this century. In answering the underlying questions of this book, I recognize that many Latina/o families in the United States are socioeconomically advantaged, professional, and wealthy, but I focus on a larger segment of the Latina/o population. I focus on the Latina/o children who face significant challenges in the United States, particularly those whose families have low incomes and primarily speak Spanish. That segment, which is now spread over a larger number of cities and states than in the past, is one that the contemporary expansion of early childhood education is trying to reach and that national debates about early childhood education often highlight explicitly or implicitly.

The Convergence of National Trends in Texas

These three nationwide trends and the often contentious debates associated with them are playing out in Texas, which has a surprisingly long history of emphasizing early childhood education and is home to a substantial share of the Latina/o population in this country. Many people, including me, would say Texas is hardly a paragon for other states to emulate in some ways. However, it is a bellwether state in terms of population change and implications for that change in the education system. As a bellwether, Texas needs to be studied carefully for lessons other states can follow and pitfalls other states can avoid. A closer look at this state I call home shows some of the advances and challenges in the Texas public education system.

Early Intervention, Accountability, and the Children of Texas

Texas has long been a leader in the state-funded expansion of early childhood educational opportunities. That is an intriguing story that began in the 1980s with a state commission on public education led by the billionaire and later presidential candidate H. Ross Perot. Appointed by a Democratic governor, Perot convened a panel of experts, led a series of meetings in schools across the state, and worked with a team of lobbyists to develop wide-ranging legislation targeting areas of advancement in Texas education as a means of improving the state's large and growing workforce. The legislation that resulted had many controversial elements, including reapportioning money across district lines, implementing competency tests for teachers, and barring academically struggling students from playing school sports (even football! In Texas!). One less controversial piece was the ambitious goal to create Texas's own version of Head Start, specifically, a school-linked public pre-K program for students from selected groups considered at risk for academic problems. Not only did this legislation pass, including the early childhood education component, it was funded by a large tax increase, which seems incredible given the antitax climate of Texas today. That was the start of the Texas public prekindergarten initiative, providing free early childhood education for four-year-olds from special populations of interest, such as low-income families, homeless families, English language learners, foster care, and active-duty military families. The initiative is supported by funding from the state and from local school districts (Chira, 1992; National Institute of Early Education Research [NIEER], 2013).

That public pre-K experiment has grown and changed over the years. It is now quite large, serving nearly 400,000 children in addition to another 60,000 in Head Start, representing 49 percent of the Texas population of four-year-olds; a much larger, albeit hard to calculate, number of Texas four-year-olds meet eligibility requirements. With that enormous reach, Texas is one of the top states in children's access to affordable early childhood education, but its per child spending on this level of education still ranks in the lower half of states. The quality of the program has also been debated, often in terms of a false "hard versus soft" approach to early teaching and learning. As the birthplace of No Child Left Behind, Texas has been a site of a standards and accountability push in early childhood education. The state program has generally been characterized by a whole-child philosophy emphasizing a range of developmental domains such as health and social skills and triangulated between community, family, and school. The Texas initiative also has been supplemented with a series of increasingly concrete plans to enrich the curricula of pre-K programs associated with school districts in order to specify the academic skills children need to exhibit to be considered school-ready, to professionalize the workforce of teachers, and to more rigorously assess effectiveness through test scores. In general, these efforts have been in service to the goal of making early childhood education in Texas more academic (Landry et al., 2009; Landry et al., 2011; NIEER, 2013, 2017; Texas Education Agency [TEA], 2017, 2018).

The degree to which such changes to the Texas program and the program itself are working is still an open question, and the potential answers to this question crystallize what is happening on the national level. Echoing evaluations of Head Start and other programs, longitudinal studies of children enrolled in the Texas pre-K program tend to show immediate benefits, with children scoring higher on a battery of school readiness assessments to a substantial degree, followed by a fade-out across most academic areas as they move through public schools, then the emergence of new benefits on long-term educational trajectories such as on-time high school graduation and college enrollment. There are fade-out effects on academic achievement that are then matched with "sleeper" effects on educational attainment (TEA, 2016, 2017). The program is working, perhaps not in the way that is expected or to the degree that is hoped. There is something to build on and a need to improve.

This state public pre-k program was created by a Democratic governor who promptly was booted from office in part from the furor over the whole of Perot's educational reforms, but it has been taken up by some subsequent governors from across the aisle, including George W. Bush before he departed Austin for Washington, DC. Republican Governor Greg Abbott rededicated the state to early childhood education to much fanfare upon his election in 2014. Interestingly, he did so despite strong pushback from some in his party who argued that there was no evidence that early education actually improves the academic fortunes of children or really repays its costs but also that it is a threat to conservative values. Indeed, some of Abbott's own backers decried his investment in public pre-K as creeping socialism and as a Godless encroachment on family autonomy. His economic message that an investment in children is an investment in the future workforce won the day (Collier, 2016; Severns, 2014).

The state's public pre-K program has been complemented by newer legislation aiming to increase the quality of public pre-K through a more academic curriculum aligned with school readiness goals in reading, writing, language, and mathematics, as well as more professional training and development for teachers and more rigorous student monitoring. This Texas experiment mirrors the construction of similar public pre-K programs in other states such as Georgia and Oklahoma that are politically conservative and free market–oriented but not historically Latina/o states that do have growing Latina/o populations (Cascio & Schanzenbach, 2013; Gormley et al., 2005). That means the pre-K push connects what is going on in established destination states with high Latina/o representation for many decades to newer destination states where low Latina/o representation as recently as the 1990s is followed by significant increases in the Latina/o population (Lichter & Johnson, 2009; Massey, 2008).

Thus, Texas has been among several very similar and somewhat similar states pioneering the expansion of access to early childhood education; its state program is now at a flashpoint in debates over how to improve quality once that expansion has happened.

Demography as Destiny in Texas

The first official state demographer of Texas and later US Census Bureau director, Steve Murdock, once told a reporter that "the Texas of today is the U.S. of tomorrow" (in Hamilton, 2010). Murdock explained that Texas is frequently on the leading edge of demographic change in the country. Because it is, it must wrestle with the challenges and opportunities of such change, including in education, years before the rest of the country does. Other states can look to Texas to see what awaits them and decide what to do and what not to do.

This leading-edge position of Texas is clearly the case in the Latinization of the United States. Given how close it is to Mexico and its role as a gateway into the United States from Latin America, Texas is considered an established destination for Latina/o immigrants and their descendants. As an established destination, policy makers in many of the newer destination states like Georgia and Iowa look to see the potential effects of the growth of their own Latina/o populations. US Census data show that the Texas population is about 40 percent Latina/o, more than double the Latina/o representation in the United States as a whole and more than triple the Latina/o representation in many states most commonly cited as new destinations.[1] Yet, Census Bureau population projections indicate that by 2050 the expected growth of the Latina/o population in the United States over the next three decades will be four times that population's growth in Texas. The Latinization of Texas has plateaued, but the Latinization of the country, largely in the newer destination states, will continue apace for some time. The other states have a long way to go to catch up to Texas in Latina/o population, but they are moving steadily in that direction.

The influence of Latina/o residents on Texas culture has been enormous, but this share of the state's population also has high rates of residential segregation, linguistic isolation, and poverty and faces a good deal of discrimination in everyday life and in societal institutions. Even accounting for the great diversity among Latina/o Americans in Texas, they are often characterized as being disadvantaged relative to the general population of the state.

Such population change and its related disadvantages for Latina/o Americans are clearly evident among Texas children in general and within the educational system in particular. Of the nearly seven million children in Texas, the majority are now Latina/o. Although Texas is a majority-minority state overall, meaning that less than 50 percent of the full population is white, it is not a majority Latina/o state, as whites still make up the largest share. However, the child population is now majority Latina/o, which speaks to the future demographic profile of the state as a whole. Notably, one-third of children in

---

1. Population statistics were derived from the US Census American Fact Finder online database. Fact Finder has been decommissioned and the data archived at https://data.census.gov/cedsci/.

Texas have at least one immigrant parent, primarily but not exclusively from Mexico and Central America, although almost all those children are US citizens themselves. The Latina/o proportion of public school students in Texas is even higher and growing more rapidly. On average, Latina/o students are less likely to complete high school or take advanced coursework, and they score lower on achievement tests across the K-12 system. Poverty is a significant contributing factor, as Latina/o children are more likely than other Texas children to live in low-income families, attend schools in high-poverty areas, and suffer many of the hardships that go along with poverty, such as lack of health insurance, underfunded and overburdened services, and exposure to crime (Center for Public Policy Priorities, 2016; Texas Demographic Center, 2016; Tienda, 2009; US Census Bureau, 2018).

Like many other states, Texas has pitched its early childhood education program at groups of children considered to be vulnerable in some way, although any Texas child may attend a public pre-K program for a fee. Given that two of the largest vulnerable groups targeted by the state's pre-K program are children from low-income families and English language learners, two groups in which Latina/o Americans are overrepresented, Latina/o children make up the greatest share of children in the program. Still, there are many Latina/o children who are not enrolled in the state program or any early childhood education program at all. When they enter kindergarten, a smaller percentage of Latina/o children (53%) are considered to be school-ready according to official standardized assessments than in the full population of young Texans (59%) (TEA, 2016).

Texas has many young Latina/o children who come from a diverse array of backgrounds but collectively have above-average odds of experiencing hardship and disadvantage and, reflecting that, demonstrate below-average academic performance. Moreover, although the state has made progress in expanding access to early childhood education, it has not closed achievement gaps early in the K-12 system between Latina/o children and many other groups of children. The experiences of this heavily Latina/o state potentially forecast similar struggles for the educational systems in a country that is becoming increasingly Latina/o and similar challenges for an economy, culture, and political system so strongly influenced by the educational system.

A Texas School District as a Window into US Education

The need for a holistic approach to learning and development when serving the most vulnerable children validates the importance of continuing the contemporary trend toward early childhood education for more children in the United States. I also question whether developmentally appropriate practices and standards-based approaches really are either/or propositions. I explore this argument with rich data from a large urban school district in Texas, pseudonymously referred to here as the Southwestern Independent School District (SWISD), that provides an important window into national debates about early education and their crystallization in the state of Texas.

Introducing Southwest Independent School District

If modern Texas offers a valuable window into national debates over early childhood education in a society with an increasing Latina/o population, then SWISD and its surrounding community are a microcosm of modern Texas in many ways. There are two reasons SWISD is a specific place to look for a more general story, both having to do with the rule and some exceptions to the rule.

The first reason is contextual. SWISD is located in one of the fastest-growing metropolitan areas in the country; it is a good representation of a largely urban country with big cities characterized by increasing racial/ethnic and linguistic diversity as well as high levels of economic inequality. In particular, its large Latina/o community, well over a third of the total population of the city, is where some big cities are right now and where many others will soon be. Much like the demographic comparison of Texas and the rest of the country, the Latina/o representation in this city is just about two times the Latina/o representation of the United States as a whole. Yet, the much slower growth of the Latina/o population in the city than in the United States over the coming decades means that the rest of the country, especially newer destination states, will be closing the gap.[2]

Accordingly, the school district serving this city is also large and diverse, with just under 90,000 total students, of whom the majority are Latina/o and more than a quarter are English language learners, mostly Spanish-speaking. Comparing district to city reveals that the Latina/o composition of SWISD is 20 percentage points greater than even the sizeable Latina/o composition of the broader city in which SWISD is situated. Such a demographic difference between district and city is common in many large metropolitan areas of the United States, primarily due to white flight from urban school districts and other forces of racial/ethnic segregation within the edu-

---

2. The demographic and educational information in this section comes from reports of the city and school district that I do not name explicitly in the book.

cational system. Thus, SWISD reflects the broader trend toward predominantly minority districts serving much more diverse cities, but it also stands out when looking at this general rule. Specifically, this demographic difference is much less pronounced in this city than in many others; in other words, SWISD has historically done a better job than many other districts in and out of Texas of keeping a more representative, albeit not actually representative, share of the city's population within its schools. Still, SWISD is far more Latina/o than most school districts in the country if not the state, even urban ones. The point is that other districts and cities are moving closer demographically to SWISD and its home city; SWISD is not moving closer to them.

The second reason is educational. SWISD has long capitalized on the Texas pre-K movement to offer early childhood education in many of its elementary schools. The district now has pre-K enrollment north of 6,000 four-year-olds, and half of all of the kindergarten students in the district attended a public pre-K program within the district, usually in the same school. The majority of children in the early childhood education program are Latina/o and/or come from low-income families, and more than a third are English language learners. Notably, the Latina/o representation of the early childhood education program is slightly lower than for the K-12 student population. That means SWISD is serving large numbers of Latina/o children, but they are still underrepresented in this optional enrollment program compared to the levels of schooling in which enrollment is mandatory. SWISD has rapidly expanded its early childhood education program over the years but seemingly without extensive centralized planning. It is spread across scores of elementary schools with different approaches to learning and development; that has heterogeneous effects on children's academic skill development as measured by standardized tests, with about 65 percent of graduates testing as school-ready, which, admittedly, can be viewed in glass half full or glass half empty terms. In these ways, SWISD is well aligned with the norm of urban school districts attempting to offer early childhood education to help children get a leg up on school.

One aspect that made SWISD stand apart is that during my time conducting research there in the early 2010s, some schools had pre-K classrooms on site, while limitations in their physical capacities to house pre-K classrooms led other schools to house those classrooms in a single, large pre-K campus that I refer to as Cole Pre-K Campus. About 650 children were dropped off at their official elementary schools every morning and then bused to Cole for the day. There they were completely surrounded by other four-year-olds, and their teachers were surrounded by other early education teachers. At the same time, young children in the other schools spent the day surrounded by older children, and their teachers were immersed in staffs of primarily K-5 teachers. This peculiarity created an interesting natural experiment in which different delivery systems of early childhood education could be compared to help understand what works best. Overall, I would call SWISD both vibrant and struggling, innovative in some ways but stagnant in others, and reflective of cities in general while also maintaining a few interesting quirks.

On the Ground in the District

In SWISD, young children spend a full day in their pre-K programs. In these programs they receive either monolingual English or bilingual, usually English and Spanish, instruction in language and literacy, math, social studies, science, health, and the arts, with time set aside for physical education, play, rest, breakfast, and lunch. They are overseen by several hundred teachers who, departing from the norm for early childhood educators in general, are college graduates. Many have achieved certification in child development, bilingual instruction, and other special services for and approaches to teaching young children.

Working with SWISD officials, I identified elementary schools within the district that had pre-K programs and selected nine schools for a closer look based on variable Latina/o representation and whether the pre-K classes were on site or at Cole.[3] Once these schools were selected, my graduate students and I spent a lot of time in them. Informally, I would say that we watched and talked. We, of course, did not do so without any kind of plan. There were definitely things that we were watching for and talking about, particularly the activities that teachers led in the classrooms, their general pedagogical approaches and behaviors, the interactions between children and teachers, and the general engagement of children. Still, we also kept our eyes open to get a good feel for what these classrooms were like and how they were experienced. In the process, we were trying to discern whether this feel differed across classrooms that had different student demographics or were housed in different kinds of schools. Understanding the convergence where things are similar and where they differ can tell a story.

3. Balancing the scope of the sample with the feasibility of in-school data collection, the total number of schools identified for participation was 12. Three of those schools, however, ended up not participating, mostly out of concerns about intrusions into classroom activities. There were no clear differences between these schools and the nine that did participate.

For the watching part, we had a good deal of unstructured time in which we observed children, teachers, and the goings-on of classrooms, and we matched this unstructured time with a more focused and systematic type of observation. My students and I were trained and certified in a protocol for standardized classroom observation that is called the Classroom Assessment Scoring System, CLASS (Pianta, La Paro, & Hamre, 2007), which is one of the major assessment tools used by Head Start and many other public pre-K programs that require evaluation as a condition of federal or state funding.[4] The CLASS provides quantitative ratings of the quality of the classroom learning environment across subject areas, emphasizing interaction processes rather than the content of a physical environment, materials, or curriculum. It involves a systematic observe/record schedule over two hours, in which raters are cued to look for and assess teacher-student interactions, teacher behaviors, and student behaviors on specific dimensions of classroom quality during short windows of time. They spend several minutes rating the classroom on each of these dimensions using a seven-point scale (low to high) along with recording informative notes about their observations. They repeat this cycle several times to capture the different kinds of classroom dynamics that unfold over time.

As shown in table I.1, the CLASS has three main dimensions of classroom quality that are each broken down into a few subdimensions, which are then measured according to sets of finer-grained indicators. The three main dimensions and their associated subdimensions are emotional support (climate, teacher sensitivity, regard for student progress), classroom organization (behavior management, productivity, instrumental learning), and instructional support (quality of feedback, conceptual development, language modeling).

Once we completed the CLASS cycles in a classroom on a given school day, we averaged the ratings for all subdimensions to come up with a final rating for each quality dimension and then averaged the three quality dimensions into a final rating of total classroom quality. Combining these various ratings with our more detailed notes about what we observed in classrooms, we then created a holistic picture of each classroom that mixed both academic and socioemotional dynamics. We also supplemented these classroom observations with records about the class such as its racial/ethnic composition and proportion of English language learners as well as the ag-

---

4. The reliability and validity of the CLASS have been thoroughly vetted at the national level (Pianta, Belsky, Houts, et al., 2007), and it has been used effectively in a wide array of studies of preschool children of low-income families (Burchinal et al., 2010; Domínguez et al., 2011; Vitiello, 2013; Wasik & Hindman, 2011).

Table I.1. Breakdown of dimensions of the CLASS

Emotional support	*Classroom organization*	*Instructional support*
Positive climate Relationships Positive affect Positive communication Respect	*Behavior management* Clear behavior expectations Proactive Redirection of misbehavior Student behavior	*Concept development* Analysis and reasoning Creating Integrating Connections to the real world
Negative climate Negative affect Punitive control Sarcasm, disrespect Severe negativity	*Productivity* Maximizing learning time Routines Transitions Preparation	*Quality of feedback* Scaffolding Feedback loops Promoting through processes Providing information Encouragement and affirmation
Teacher sensitivity Awareness Responsiveness Addresses problems Student comfort	*Instructional learning formats* Effective facilitation Variety of modalities and materials Student interest Clarity of learning objectives	*Language modeling* Frequent conversation Open-ended questions Repetition and extension Self and parallel talk Advanced language
Regard for students' perspective Flexibility and student focus Support for autonomy and leadership Student expression Restriction of movement		

gregate academic performance of the classroom such as the proportion of students testing as school-ready by the end of the school year.

Given that I often felt sensory overload in the noise and activity of classrooms, the CLASS helped me get a grip and better discern what was actually going on in front of me. In that way, it was a real anchor in the data collection. That does not mean the CLASS is without limitations, and many of its limitations are directly relevant to the study of Latina/o children from low-income families. For one, although there is evidence that the CLASS is a reliable tool in different countries and sociodemographic groups, its findings need to be interpreted with the appropriate caveats that the CLASS was not designed to study Latina/o children or classrooms in which activities are not solely conducted in English (Campaign for Quality Early Education Coalition, 2013; Vitiello 2013). Another limitation is that although the CLASS covers many domains of classroom activity, it is certainly not exhaustive, and what is left out might matter to the study of Latina/o children. Efforts to design similar classroom observational protocols in Mexico, for example, highlight domains that speak to the value of classroom activities that are directly tied to children's experiences in their own communities and groups (Jensen et al., 2018). Still, I consider the CLASS a good tool for getting a grasp on what the classrooms populated by young Latina/o children from low-income families are like, but I acknowledge that it is not perfect. That is precisely why I did not stop with the watching part.

For the talking part, we had many conversations with teachers, administrators, parent-support specialists, and parents while also listening to children as they went about their day, but we again matched this unstructured talk with a more systematic approach to listening and learning. In each classroom that we observed, we also conducted semistructured interviews with teachers and teaching assistants. These interviews were intended to reveal the complex processes that might be underlying instructional quality that would otherwise be unknown or captured in much less depth in the kinds of large-scale quantitative data often used in studies of educational policy and practice.[5] The goal was to delve into topics of interest while also allowing room for new topics to emerge, to provide a basic guide but also let the interviews go on their own. Thus, we had an interview guide that included prompts for basic discussion points and specific questions but allowed flexibility for follow-up questions and exploration of emerging top-

---

5. All teachers were assured complete anonymity, signed consent forms, were allowed to choose the language of the interview, and were compensated with $40. Interviews were audio-recorded and transcribed.

Table I.2. Segments and sample questions from the teacher interview guide

Segment	Sample questions
Teacher background	1. What got you into teaching? How did you arrive at this job, and what is your motivation for staying in the job? 2. What kind of teaching certification do you have? Do you think the certification process was useful for you, and how has it prepared you or not for what you actually do in class?
Classroom dynamics	1. Walk me through your typical day as a teacher, from before kids arrive until after they leave. Do you think this is different from what most teachers in this grade in SWISD do? 2. Tell me, in your own words, what makes a classroom good or not? What defines success to you when you evaluate your students at the end of the year? Would your answers to these questions be different if you had students from different backgrounds in your class?
Integration and coordination	1. Do you feel like, as a teacher, you are in it alone, or do you feel part of a larger community of teachers who work together as a team? Who is your community/team? 2. How self-contained is your classroom? By that, we mean how much your classroom is linked to other classrooms in the school. What form do these links take? Do they emerge from teachers' interactions, or are they shaped from the top down by school administrators? Is there some official policy, and if so, does it matter?

ics.[6] This guide was broken up into three segments; table I.2 presents a selection of sample questions from each segment).

The first of these three segments of the guide, *teacher background*, focused on the teacher's educational and professional history (degrees, certification, work history, tenure in position and school, teacher training and professional development) and on her or his classroom and students (curricular design, approach to instruction, student skill levels).

The second segment, *classroom dynamics*, focused on challenges and op-

---

6. This process for conducting a qualitative study is related to the grounded theory tradition of social science, in which theory is inductively developed through the collection and analysis of data. Using some a priori starting points but allowing insights to emerge helps to iteratively identify and develop new concepts (Charmaz, 2006).

portunities perceived by teachers specific to the predominant child group in the classroom (low-income versus low-income English language learners), including experiences with the school and district in meeting these challenges or capitalizing on these opportunities.

The third segment, *integration and coordination*, focused on how teachers work with other teachers across classrooms and within and across grade levels to maintain or improve the quality of the learning and developmental environment for children and how the teachers do or do not get support from the school and district in this endeavor.

In general, my students and I used these interviews to first build rapport and then to dig deeper. They were scheduled for an hour apiece, but they often went far longer and occasionally led to sequel conversations. I definitely got the sense that for many teachers, these interviews were the first time they had been asked what they felt and thought.[7]

For the subset of pre-K classrooms located at the Cole Pre-K Campus, we coupled teacher interviews with similar interviews with a parent of a student in each classroom. All but three of these mothers were Latina/o, with most speaking Spanish as a first language and some as the only language. These interviews were wider-ranging than the interviews with teachers and focused more on what was happening outside the classroom and school. Some of these conversations, however, focused on what parents thought their children were getting at school, how they interacted with their children's teachers, and what they wanted from those teachers. These conversations occurred in group settings and individually, often in Spanish.

All of this watching and talking could then be systematically integrated to generate important insights that I will cover in depth in the chapters.[8] As

---

7. The interviews and observation notes proved to be a veritable wealth of information, almost to the point of being overwhelming. To make sense of what we had while following the grounded theory tradition, I developed a formal protocol for systematically analyzing these data based on conventional qualitative practices (Miles & Huberman, 1984; Ryan & Bernard, 2003). My students and I hand-coded sample transcripts and field notes with cut-and-sort procedures and then discussed the overlap and differences in the themes we had coded, both themes we went in expecting to see and those that emerged more organically. We used this activity to create a codebook to guide the final coding of all materials with the NVivo software. With this software we organized materials under themes, cross-classified by classroom type, classroom location, and teacher background.

8. This combination of quantitative (CLASS) and qualitative (interview) data is mostly closely aligned with the mixed methods sequential explanatory design, in which a single study collects and analyzes quantitative and qualitative data in consecutive phases (Ivankova et al., 2006). In this study, however, neither the quantitative nor

background here, though, we ended up engaging in both sets of activities in a total of 58 classrooms in the nine selected SWISD schools from late 2010 through early 2012. Because of our focus on early childhood education within public schools, we did so for all 36 pre-K classrooms across these schools. In light of the influence of the PK-3 movement, emphasizing how early childhood education should be viewed as part of a trajectory across the transition into formal school, we supplemented these pre-K activities by also collecting the same data in randomly selected classrooms in kindergarten (8), first grade (8), and second grade (6) within these same schools. In other words, we paid attention to where children experienced pre-K in SWISD and then where most of them would go to school after finishing pre-K.

In this full set of pre-K, kindergarten, first grade, and second grade classrooms, 95 percent of the teachers were female, and two-thirds were Latina/o, with the remainder primarily white. Well over half of these classrooms involved primarily Spanish-language activities, taught by both Latina/o and white teachers, with a decline in the proportion of such classrooms across grade levels. Given this preponderance of Spanish-speaking classrooms, including many in which teachers preferred to talk with us in Spanish, we used bilingual versions of the CLASS and the interview guide led by members of my team who could also speak Spanish.[9]

The Goals for Spending Time in the District

The point of this watching and talking was to distill some concrete lessons from the process of answering the underlying questions of this study: What about early childhood education for Latina/o children is working, and what needs to be improved? To that end, I approached collecting and interpreting these data using a guiding model, based on past theory and research from developmental science and other disciplines, especially a perspective called contextual systems. That perspective emphasizes how the transition into elementary school among children from historically disadvantaged groups needs to be understood at the intersection of their own diverse needs and

---

qualitative data phase was prioritized, and the integration of the two sources of data primarily came in the interpretation of results after both phases were conducted instead of using insights from one source to design the collection of the second source.

9. As alluded to already, two of these graduate students, Claude Bonazzo and Aida Ramos, also helped me organize and interpret the data for some of the chapters of this book and in some cases helped to draft them, and their assistance in these chapters will be explicitly noted.

the various contexts in which they live. In this way, it situates early childhood education classrooms in the year prior to formal school entry within children's school contexts and out-of-school contexts while also breaking down their classroom experiences into different learning and developmental dynamics. By doing so, I hoped to test the proposition that children from low-income Latina/o families will have more positive experiences in a public pre-K program when their classrooms are in conversation with rather than isolated from their schools, families, and communities and when these classrooms involve a broad rather than narrow range of learning opportunities. Such children have access to early childhood education already, so maybe a system in conversation is what they need to truly gain from that access.

Working from this guiding model, I have organized the study around two main goals in answering the questions of what is working and what needs improvement in early childhood education of Latina/o children. The first aim was to explore the learning environments of young children from low-income Latina/o families at the intersection of their early childhood education classrooms and the other contexts they traverse in and out of school. I found that pre-K classrooms in SWISD were often isolated from the K-12 system. This form of pre-K segregation seemed to increase innovation at the pre-K level but reduce consistency and coordination in educational trajectories across the transition into elementary school. I also found that despite a great deal of talk about family-school-community partnerships in SWISD, several factors impeded open exchanges among teachers, Latina/o parents, and Latina/o community members. As a result, the many strengths of families and communities that early childhood education programs and elementary schools could capitalize on to better serve students often went untapped.

The second aim was to explore the learning environments of young children from low-income Latina/o families at the intersection of different philosophies about the intended outcomes of early childhood education and the divergent classroom-based activities related to these philosophies. Although most of the pre-K classrooms in SWISD could be characterized as socially and emotionally healthy places for children, most could not be characterized as having commensurate levels of cognitive stimulation and academic enrichment. Consequently, young Latina/o children in these classrooms might not gain all that they could from early childhood education. Partly this lack of well-roundedness in classrooms serving Latina/o children occurred because the perceived challenges of helping Latina/o children from Spanish-speaking households learn English interfered with teachers' engagement in other academically enriching activities with them. In these circumstances, young Latina/o children could then lose academic ground to peers because they are not getting the same kinds of instruction.

To summarize, I went into this experience looking at connections within the early childhood education of low-income Latina/o children from predominantly Spanish-speaking homes; that is, I looked at how the classrooms attempting to boost their future prospects were connected within and outside the school and how the different pieces of their classrooms were connected. In these SWISD schools, I found many such connections that model what needs to be done in the future, but I also found many disconnects that serve as warnings about how such future efforts could be undercut. Both sets of insights are important as the population of young Latina/o children from low-income families continues to increase and spreads out across the United States.

Setting the Stage

With the information gleaned from observations, interviews, and activities in SWISD, I use this study to tell a story. Before getting into that story, I want to share a few qualifiers to better put this work in context.

Defining What This Research Is and Is Not

First, the research in this book covers issues like hardship, conflict, and cultural misunderstanding, but it is ultimately about assets in the Latina/o population rather than deficits. Over the years of doing work as a scholar studying Latina/o children and families, I have become acutely aware of how the framing of such research can be misleading or even harmful, casting an unfavorable light even when that is far from the intention. Research in this area has long been guided by a focus on what is wrong and what Latina/o families are not doing (deficits) rather than a focus on what is right and what Latina/o families are doing (assets). That is especially true in research on the intersection of families and schools in the United States. Many years in and lessons learned, I try very hard to avoid falling into that trap, which is why I intend the research in this book to capture a realistic view of Latina/o children and families that recognizes disadvantages and obstacles without defining them through that lens. It is about what low-income Latina/o children and parents want and need and are trying to do and how educators do not always see that clearly.

Second, the research in this book is system-focused rather than person-focused, even though the people surely shine through the data. I use a theory about how different social systems such as families, schools, classrooms, and communities come together to shape the space in which children grow and learn, parents and teachers meet, and advantages and disadvantages intersect. I did not study individual children themselves but rather their schools and classrooms, where they and the adults in their lives connect or not as a group. That focus is important for informing policy intervention, which typically targets systemic change rather than individual change. Yet, a systems focus does not preclude hearing from or learning about individual parents and teachers or mean children are somehow absent from the data; their behaviors and interactions with adults are at the very heart of the observations we used to characterize classrooms.

Third, the research in this book is a case study with national implications but not a national study on its own. Although I learned a great deal during my time at SWISD, I did not want to learn just about SWISD. I was searching for a deeper understanding of early childhood education, particularly public programs serving young Latina/o children from low-income families. Consequently, a fair question to ask is "How much can we learn about early childhood education from one set of schools in one district in one state?" One response to this question is to go back to the idea that the Texas of today is the United States of tomorrow. I can go even further to say that as a large, fast-growing, unequal metropolitan area with a sizeable Latina/o population and an ambitious early childhood education program, the city that SWISD serves is today what Texas is tomorrow. In these ways, this district in this state is where questions need to be asked and explored right now, with whatever insights can come from that asking and exploring that are likely relevant to a much broader swath of the United States every day. Another response to this question is what might be called "benchmarking" or "calibration." With those words, I mean that when possible and data allow, I draw on national statistics about early childhood education, including the CLASS assessments from those programs across the country. That use of data will help me to figure out how much what I saw in SWISD captures what is happening in Texas and the United States and how much it is an outlier.

Overall, I would argue that this theoretically driven and empirically based research uses SWISD findings to consider the educationally supportive systems of early childhood education and the institutional rather than personal challenges to the success of those systems. Analysis shows how the findings fit with or stand out from the national norm as well as in relation to other and often more traditional perspectives.

The Story Unfolds

The story this study reveals is about a plan for early childhood education that is not always sufficiently realized because of on-the-ground challenges to the integration of schools, families, and communities and to multidimensional and developmentally informed academic experiences in the classroom. In turn, this story speaks to an actionable plan for improving the degree to which early childhood education in large urban districts in Texas can better serve the large, growing, and generally disadvantaged and often threatened low-income Latina/o population. This visible Texas case can then influence the rest of the country as it heads in the same direction in ways that point early childhood education research toward new angles to explore, inform early childhood education practice in Texas, and position Texas as a crucible for early childhood education success in the emerging demographic reality of the whole United States. Doing so can help everyone involved collectively get it right at the starting line, where it counts the most.

CHAPTER 1

The Importance of Connections in Early Childhood Education

To approach early education for the large, growing, and important population of young Latina/o children from low-income families in the United States, I identified a diverse urban district in Texas as a valuable window into this big issue. Even within that narrower window, however, a blueprint or map is necessary to pare down the scope and carve out specific points of entry. A carefully constructed blueprint for action helps in developing an in-depth understanding of some of the important pieces that make up the whole. That process can lead to significant progress in the ultimate goal of putting all the pieces together.

As a social scientist, my go-to way to construct such a blueprint is to rely on theory, that is, general sets of ideas and principles that capture the nature of some phenomenon and offer perspective on it. More specifically, I am a developmental scientist and a sociologist. Integrating these two sides of my scientific self, I often draw upon developmental theory infused with sociological insights such as perspectives that place children's development within context to construct blueprints for action when I set out to study an educational or societal issue involving children and their families.

If theory is the key to constructing a blueprint and developmental theory is where I tend to look for guidance in doing so, then what does developmental theory have to say about studying the early education of young Latina/o children from low-income families in the United States? More to the point, what developmental theory is relevant to understanding how early childhood education is serving the needs of such children or instead missing the mark, and how can that theoretically guided understanding support the articulation of mechanisms for improving early childhood education as a system moving forward?

For me, the answer to these questions begins with a perspective called "contextual systems theory," which is an education-focused offshoot of a broader theoretical perspective on child development called "systems theory."[1] The basic point is that children grow up and learn within a complex set of give and take between the different parts of their lives and the contexts in which they live their lives. Consequently, figuring out what is helping them and what may hurt them must start with an exploration of that give and take. That is true in general but especially for the transition from early childhood education into elementary school. Moreover, it holds for children from all walks of life but particularly for children from historically disadvantaged and disenfranchised groups. My blueprint takes this basic idea of give and take, which I call connections, and applies it to the specific experiences of the many young Latina/o children in the United States for whom early childhood education could be a springboard for a better tomorrow.

In this chapter, therefore, I lay out the developmental theory that guided me in this study of such a big issue and then offer the theoretically informed blueprint that pointed me to particular parts of this big issue on which to focus that study. Each piece of that blueprint then inspired one specific chapter of this book.[2]

Theories on Children in Need in Early Childhood Education

Children are wonderfully complex creatures, and they develop this complexity within specific locations made up of overlapping social, cultural, and economic contexts that are equally complex. Capturing that complexity is crucial to understanding both the child (in this case, young Latina/o children from low-income families) and the context (in this case, early childhood education). Advances in developmental theories over the past several decades provide the tools to make sense of all of that complexity and study it directly.

---

1. I know that some do not like the term "systems" because it sounds more like machinery than child development, but to be consistent with the theory, I will use the conventional systems language here in setting up the blueprint but then shift to other language as I discuss the actual blueprint and the research it guided.

2. Using a clear but flexible starting point that guided the approach to data collection, which then informed the continual development and refinement of core concepts and ideas, this study fell into the grounded theory tradition.

Developmental Systems Theory

The general developmental systems perspective is one of the most prominent theories of contemporary research on child development. In some ways, it arose as a critique of traditional developmental theories for being "undersocialized." In other words, there was emerging consensus that many such theories focused too much on children's growth, maturation, and acquisition of cognitive and socioemotional skills and not enough on the social environments in which children live that powerfully influence how they grow, mature, and acquire skills and that differentiate the developmental pathways of some children from other children over time. To "socialize" traditional developmental models, systems theory emphasizes the bidirectional transactions between children and their environments. The term "bidirectional transactions" refers to the back and forth between two things, with each side influencing the other rather than one side always being the influencer and the other being the influenced. That means that just as some environment influences the child, the child also influences that environment. For example, parenting, as a key dimension of the home environment, guides children's behavioral development, such as when children who receive harsh or cold parenting begin to exhibit aggressive behaviors. We also know that aggressive children tend to elicit harsher treatment from parents. In this way, the environmental effect (parenting influencing child behavior) and the child effect (child behavior influencing parenting) are intertwined and mutually reinforcing over time. That is a bidirectional transaction (Lerner, 2006; Sameroff, 1983).

Importantly, systems are not completely external to the child; one can also think of environmental systems within the body. Transactions, then, occur between and across the inside of the child and the outside of the child. All of these systems are arranged in a kind of hierarchy from the most micro level to the most macro level. Biological systems within the child such as the circulatory system and organs are embedded within the child herself or himself, who is embedded in social systems that are quite concrete and immediate (families, schools), which are embedded in broad cultural and structural systems that are more abstract and distal (social class, history). Transactions between systems, within and across these various levels of hierarchy, organize children's development and maximize the two-way adaptation between children and their environments. Imbalances or conflicts within this full set of systems, therefore, are maladaptive and can lead to developmental problems (Cox & Paley, 1997; Yoshikawa & Hsueh, 2001).

Systems theory is a perspective on child development in general, but it can be adapted to specific aspects of children's lives. One such specific use of the theory is in contextual systems.

Contextual Systems Theory

The focus of contextual systems theory is early childhood education and particularly learning and development across the transition from early childhood education into elementary school. Even more specifically, this theoretical perspective is geared toward the supports and risks that are often experienced by children from disadvantaged circumstances within the most significant contexts of their daily lives during this critical period of the educational career (Rimm-Kaufman & Pianta, 2000).

Because transactions among such contextual systems help to direct children's trajectories into and through elementary school, these transactions and not just the contextual systems themselves represent an important starting point for understanding and correcting the barriers that some children—disproportionately from low-income, racial/ethnic minority, and immigrant backgrounds—face at the starting line. The source of risk is not necessarily deficiencies in any one contextual system but instead in problems that arise in the connections among systems. In contextual systems theory, these problems are often referred to colloquially as a failure of communication between key contexts of children's lives. This term can be taken both literally (people in two contexts not talking with each other) and figuratively (two contexts not working well together).

What does it mean to say that the contextual systems of children's lives are or are not properly communicating? When systems are in conversation, they have multiple interactions over time so that these interactions become stable, regular, and expected. In short, they demonstrate set patterns of working in sync with each other to leverage what both have to offer each other and the child. In the process, these transactions develop into something that is superordinate to either system itself. Such conversations are effective when the whole that combines the two systems is greater than their sum. They are ineffective, even destructive, when these interactions are one-sided, unbalanced, adversarial, or apathetic. Not surprisingly, children tend to post higher rates of learning when the contexts of their lives are effectively communicating (Crosnoe, 2012; Pianta & Walsh, 1996).

More broadly, contextual systems theory asserts that ineffective communication between key contexts helps to explain why some segments of the child population are academically "at risk," where "risk" means that past empirical evidence has indicated a higher probability of poor outcomes in these segments compared to others (Eaton, 1981). In particular, two forms of ineffective communication are related to risk defined this way. First, children from at-risk groups might be challenged by problematic or nonexistent interactions between key contextual systems, such as when two contexts are not in conversation or have ineffective or damaging conversations (again, literally or figuratively). Second, children from at-risk groups have problems because the interactions within each system are asymmetrical, such as when what is going on in one system contradicts, in spirit or content, what is occurring simultaneously in the other system. These two forms of ineffective communication help to translate probabilistic risk factors into poor outcomes (Crosnoe, 2012; Pianta & Walsh, 1996).

According to contextual systems theory, therefore, the start of formal schooling is a period of the educational career in which the negative interplay or lack of positive interplay between contextual systems is most implicated in the "miseducation" of children who really need to use the educational system to get ahead. Thus, attempts to understand and do something about any kind of social, economic, or demographic disparity in educational attainment should focus on their roots in the earliest stages of schooling and consider children's educational and developmental experiences at the intersection of key contextual systems.

Focal Transactions among and within Contextual Systems

Young Latina/o children are often considered an "at-risk" group in the US educational system, as they collectively score less well on conventional markers of educational and academic achievement than does the general population of children. That is particularly true for young Latina/o children from low-income immigrant backgrounds (Crosnoe & Lopez-Turley, 2011; Hemphill et al., 2011; Krogstad, 2016; Reardon & Galindo, 2009; Stanton-Salazar, 2001). Of course, many Latina/o children do quite well in the educational system; they comprise an internally diverse group, after all. But the statistical definition of risk refers to overall odds, not actual individual outcomes. Contextual systems theory is likely to be of value when studying the current experiences and future prospects of young Latina/o children from low-income and often immigrant families.

In applying the theory to this important group of children in the United States, one can think of the early childhood education classroom as the nexus of transactions among contextual systems. The classroom is a context in and of itself, and it is also a context that exists within a larger set of concentric and overlapping contextual systems; it is located within schools and

CONTEXTUAL CONNECTIONS

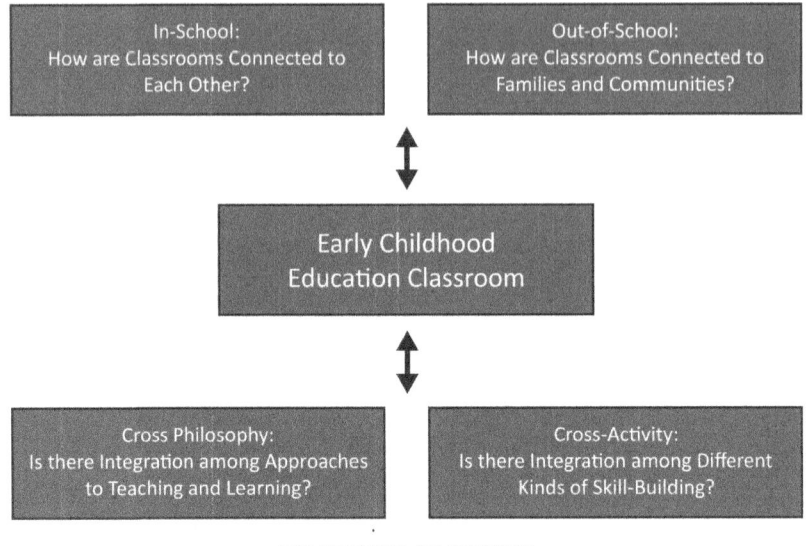

```
┌─────────────────────────────┐         ┌─────────────────────────────┐
│        In-School:           │         │       Out-of-School:        │
│ How are Classrooms Connected to │     │ How are Classrooms Connected to │
│        Each Other?          │         │  Families and Communities?  │
└─────────────────────────────┘         └─────────────────────────────┘
                                 ↕
                  ┌───────────────────────────┐
                  │     Early Childhood       │
                  │   Education Classroom     │
                  └───────────────────────────┘
                                 ↕
┌─────────────────────────────┐         ┌─────────────────────────────┐
│     Cross Philosophy:       │         │      Cross-Activity:        │
│ Is there Integration among Approaches │ │ Is there Integration among Different │
│   to Teaching and Learning? │         │   Kinds of Skill-Building?  │
└─────────────────────────────┘         └─────────────────────────────┘
```

CONNECTED PROCESSES

Figure 1.1. Blueprint derived from contextual systems theory

community. It is also a context that can be divided into its own constituent contextual systems such as activities and arrangements within the classroom that differentiate one classroom from another. Thus, what is going right and wrong for young Latina/o children from low-income families within the system of early childhood education may be considered in terms of interactions between and among what a child is exposed to inside the classroom and how that classroom is situated in that child's and her or his family's broader environments.

A Blueprint for Study and Action

Developmental systems theory begat contextual systems theory, which begat the blueprint for the research in an early childhood education program on which this book is based. Figure 1.1 presents this blueprint.

Again, this blueprint is centered on the early childhood education classrooms attended by young Latina/o children from low-income families, with such classrooms involved in transactions among other, broader contextual systems and comprised of transactions among a different set of more intimate contextual systems. In the spirit of accessibility, I will describe this blueprint while switching away from some of the jargonesque terms of theory to use more straightforward language, first and foremost replacing the somewhat clunky term "transactions" with the more commonplace "connections."

In short, this blueprint is about drawing connections in all directions around early childhood educational classrooms.

Contextual Connections

The top portion of figure 1.1 captures the connections of early childhood classrooms with other contexts that are key parts of the larger fabric of community life, in schools, families, and communities. Essentially, I want to know whether these contexts are in conversation with each other or whether they stand, actively or passively, at a remove from each other. Figure 1.2 elaborates on the contextual connections part of this blueprint. This elaboration has two basic avenues. I will describe each, including the important concepts, how I will actually use data to study these concepts, and what the policy relevance of doing so is.

First, the connections of an early childhood education classroom with other linked classrooms in schools are important to consider, as shown in the "In school" sequence in the top half of figure 1.2. In exploring those contextual connections, the key concept of interest is *alignment*. This concept refers to the active coordination of curriculum, instruction, and activities within and across grades to create a more cohesive educational experience for children transitioning from preschool into the primary grades of elementary school. Alignment among early childhood education classrooms in a school or program—with teachers working together to figure out the most effective teaching methods, plan learning activities, and support each other—can potentially help each individual classroom better serve children. Alignment between early childhood education classrooms and primary grade class-

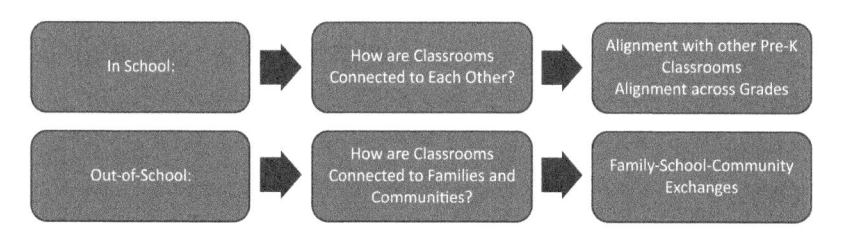

Figure 1.2. A closer look at contextual connections

rooms—with teachers working together to ensure that the former are oriented toward building a foundation for future learning opportunities and the latter are able to capitalize on that foundation—can potentially guard against fade-out of early childhood education effects and continue a trajectory of learning (Bogard & Takanishi, 2005).

Different dimensions of alignment were a key focus of the SWISD research. This line of inquiry primarily involved interviews with teachers in the dozens of pre-K, kindergarten, first grade, and second grade classrooms in SWISD as well as unstructured observations of activities in and around these classrooms. Drawing on all early childhood education classrooms in a given school and a sample of primary grade classrooms that those early childhood education classrooms fed into in each school provided a view of how teachers partner with peers in the same level of schooling and across connected levels of schooling. Of note is that the presence of the Cole Pre-K Campus in our sample of schools supported this inquiry. It offered a contrast between early childhood education classrooms separated from their children's ultimate primary grade destinations or housed on location with them. Across classrooms, regardless of level or location, teachers responded to explicit questioning about alignment activities but also spoke, unprompted, about these activities and the general philosophy behind them. My job was to organize what they said and what we observed into some general themes about when and where alignment efforts were successful and what kinds of obstacles stand in the way of such success.

The insights gained from this component of my contextual connections exploration are directly relevant to a major national policy agenda: PK-3. This agenda discourages thinking of early childhood education as separate from elementary education, which itself spans the period of rapid development and learning encompassed by the years from kindergarten through fifth grade. Instead, PK-3 proposes thinking of early childhood education and primary education (kindergarten through third grade) as part of a single stage of the larger education. The thought is that such a shift would better serve young children in developmentally appropriate ways and more effectively set them up for future achievement, but this shift requires a degree of active and purposeful alignment that is not always the norm (Kauerz, 2006; Stipek et al., 2017). Thus, figuring out where it is occurring and why it is not when it is not can support this proposed rethinking of educational policy.

Second, the connections of an early childhood education classroom to the families and communities sending their children to these classrooms are also important to consider, as shown in the "Out-of-school" sequence in the bottom half of figure 1.2. In exploring those contextual connections, the key concept of interest is *family-school-community partnership*, which refers to strong and active ties among school personnel, parents and other family members of children in the school, and community members with a stake in what happens in the school. Such partnerships are key foci of numerous educational and developmental theories; the basic idea is that children learn more and develop more positively when the adults in the major contexts of their lives are on the same team. That could be because parents effectively communicate the needs and talents of their children to the school and advocate for them at school; school personnel convey the demands and opportunities of school to families and set appropriate expectations for children and parents, while community members know what is occurring in schools, hold them accountable, and serve as brokers between families and schools. Such partnerships can be especially critical to the learning and development of young people from historically disadvantaged groups during times of transition, such as when children enter early childhood education and move from there into elementary school (Crosnoe et al., 2015; Epstein, 2018; Sheridan & Moorman Kim, 2015).

I have spent a good portion of my career as a child-, family-, and school-focused sociologist concerned with family-school-community partnerships. I have been especially interested in figuring out how they work and why they do not for children from low-income and/or immigrant families and communities. When partnerships do not work for those children, there are often incredible imbalances of power and experience among the different contexts that can lead to a lack of perspective and mutual understanding; the odds are higher that the different contexts are working from different sets of unstated assumptions (Crosnoe, 2015; Crosnoe et al., 2015). Not surprisingly, I went into my time in SWISD especially interested in these partnerships. I did so even though I was aware of the dangers of not being critical of my underlying assumptions when studying Latina/o families and US schools. I also was aware that what the families may view as supporting education is often missed or misinterpreted by teachers and administrators in the schools; key concepts of Latina/o parents' socialization of children and approaches to education may entail qualities such as *respeto* and *educación* (Reese et al., 1995; Valdés, 1996). The design of interviews with teachers, other school personnel, and parents about their beliefs and behaviors related to family-school-community partnerships and especially the analysis of that interview data were informed by a critical lens. Although I came in knowing a lot about the topic, I learned an incredible amount, especially how partnerships that seem to be working at first glance are more vulnerable and less optimal on closer inspection.

The insights gained from this component of my connected contexts exploration directly inform one of the broadest policy agendas of contemporary US education, that of building bridges between schools and their family and community constituents. Those familiar with the sweeping changes to school policy created by No Child Left Behind know that it required schools to build compacts with families and communities in a form of shared governance and insight. Other programs implemented by schools and community groups help bring families and school personnel together to talk to and learn from each other, providing a scaffolding to eventually build more formal partnerships (Epstein, 2005; Goldenberg & Light, 2009; Grant & Ray, 2018). Indeed, family-school-community partnerships have become something of a tool for schools and districts aiming to improve school performance, but building the partnerships is easier said than done.

The concepts of alignment and family-school-community partnerships capture the essence of transactions in contextual systems theory in that they emphasize the back-and-forth exchange and mutual engagement among various contexts in a child's life as a key to that child's current and future prospects in school.

Connected Processes

The bottom portion of figure 1.1 illustrates the connections among different learning and teaching processes within early childhood classrooms that tap into the kinds of lessons, activities, and pedagogies in the classroom. They too can be assessed according to how much they are or are not in conversation with each other and the extent to which different processes are complementing each other or squeezing each other out. Figure 1.3 presents the connected processes part of this blueprint.

When looking at the interplay of processes within an early childhood education classroom, a good place to start is with the tension between the developmentally appropriate practices tradition and the standards and accountability movement shown in the "Cross-philosophy" sequence in the top half of figure 1.3. This tension concerns philosophical differences guiding educational policy writ large, but it plays out every day in actual classrooms. That is its ground zero (Genishi & Dyson, 2009; Graue, 2008).

Do teachers and students interact in early childhood classrooms that focus more on holistically supporting their positive development as a means of facilitating their learning? Or do these interactions unfold in classrooms that are more focused on concrete and formal academic instruction and lessons as the mode of teaching and learning? Such questions are most often

```
Cross-Philosophy:  →  Is there Integration among Approaches to Teaching and Learning?  →  Development Appropriateness and Academic Standards

Cross-Activity:  →  Is there Integration among Different Kinds of Skill-Building?  →  Language-Building and Cognitive Stimulation
```

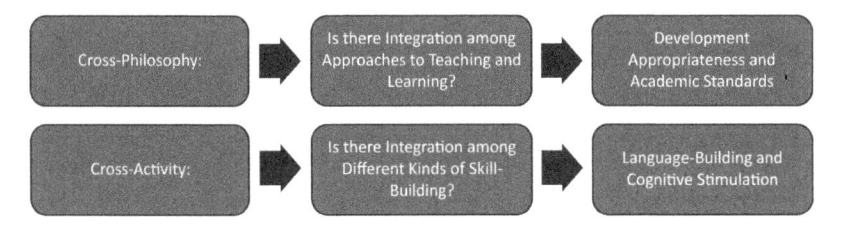

Figure 1.3. A closer look at connected processes

asked about early childhood education programs, especially federally or state-funded programs, that serve historically disadvantaged and disenfranchised groups of children; the questions are centered on the goal of figuring out the best way to promote the children's learning and future academic success. Often missed in this either/or debate is the likelihood that elements of both philosophies and practices may be mixed and matched to promote learning among children from diverse groups. The questions may be "and" rather than "either/or." More important is assessing in the real world the perception that classrooms focusing on developmentally appropriate practices are somehow devoid of academic learning and that classrooms focusing on academic standards are somehow not conducive to children's more general development.

For this assessment in SWISD I drew more heavily on the structured observations that our team conducted in early childhood education classrooms using the CLASS protocol. This protocol provided a rigorous way to look within a classroom and gain a sense of how well it is simultaneously fostering general socioemotional development and actively and purposefully stimulating the acquisition of academic skills rather than leaning more toward one of the two directions. The key was not just looking at a classroom according to one dimension or another but instead characterizing a classroom by all of the various things going on inside it at the same time. I supplemented what came out of these CLASS observations with interviews with teachers about their approaches to learning, what they want to focus on in their classrooms, and what they think they are focusing on day to day. Consistencies and inconsistencies in what we saw and what teachers say are especially useful for considering the promise and pitfalls of early childhood education.

During this time in SWISD classrooms populated by the children of low-income Latina/o families, I knew that what I was experiencing was relevant to some of the most heated debates in educational policy and practice, debates that are quite acute within the world of early childhood education and around the topic of educational inequality. In dealing with young children, after all, everyone wants to get it right even if they have very different takes on how to do that. I think the value of such research for that policy debate is giving a clear-eyed view of what is happening on the ground.

Staying within the same classroom but shifting the focus slightly, one can think of the different ways that classrooms emphasize academic learning and skill development and how these processes build off each other or not, as shown in the "Cross-activity" sequence in the bottom half of figure 1.3. This exploration of the academic side of early childhood classrooms is of heightened importance for one large subset of the Latina/o population: English language learners. Given how much the K-12 system demands English skills of students and how poorly it has served the needs of students still developing English skills, there is great pressure on early childhood educators to help English language learners enter the system with a certain degree of functionality in English. In elementary and secondary school, this pressure can be a roadblock to helping students master other kinds of academic skills, which ultimately shortchanges them. Is it because teachers do not have time for other kinds of learning, or is it because they compensate for the specific academic challenges in front of them by fostering other kinds of positive outcomes among their students such as socioemotional development? This question could be a key in efforts to help English language learners get the best start that they can, one that is intricately wrapped up with issues of developmentally appropriate practices and a standards and accountability approach (Genesee et al., 2006; Goldenberg, 2008; Karabenick & Noda, 2004; Takanishi & Le Menestrel, 2017).

For this reason, I explicitly focused on the subset of early childhood classrooms in SWISD in which instruction and learning took place mostly in Spanish. These classrooms were largely populated by the children of Latina/o immigrants and primarily led by teachers who were Latinas or Latina immigrants themselves. Whether engaging in the structured observations organized by the CLASS, more informally observing classrooms, or interviewing teachers and parents, the goal was to gain some understanding of how exactly early childhood education classrooms were helping young English language learners get ready for school. A big part of that endeavor was determining whether what was going on in these Spanish-speaking classrooms was more different than or similar to what was going on in English-speaking classrooms with Latina/o students. What might children be gaining or losing in each kind of classroom?

The policy agenda surrounding the best ways to help English language learners succeed in the US educational system has been fraught on the national level and in many states with large immigrant populations. One need only look at California to see just how fraught it can get. There, the controversial Proposition 227 mandating English-only instruction for students deemed not proficient in English was eventually softened by a new proposition after two decades of rancor. A report from the Board on Children, Youth, and Families of the US National Academy of Science (Takanishi & Le Menestrel, 2017) waded into this debate, arguing in part for a focus on the needs of young children, how to meet them, and how they are not met. I think the starting line is indeed an appropriate place to view this debate and, in the process, consider unintended consequences for how young children are taught and what they learn. That was my goal, at least, and it proved to be an eye-opening experience relevant well beyond SWISD.

The issues surrounding different kinds of teaching and learning in early childhood education programs serving young Latina/o children from low-income families are complex, challenging, and often emotional, particularly when the children in question are English language learners. That is why I approached these issues as part of a team with a combination of structured and more quantitative data and more organic and qualitative data. I wanted to use my own eyes and ears but also to place checks on myself to make sure I was not seeing and hearing what I went in expecting or wanting. That was not easy, but I will try my best to explain why it was important for what I eventually came to understand.

Putting the Blueprint to Work

Derived from developmental theory and oriented toward extant policy initiatives and debates, the blueprint for this study of early childhood education represents my attempt to marry research and action. It certainly does not cover the whole of early childhood education or encompass the entirety of Latina/o children's educational experiences in the United States. It does, however, offer the opportunity to dig into key dimensions of both issues in ways meant to directly inform educational practice. I iteratively go through this blueprint and describe the insights that I uncovered by following it during my time in SWISD. That experience offers lessons that speak to what is going on, and what should be going on, at the starting line in SWISD, in Texas, and in the United States more broadly.

CHAPTER 2

Connecting Classrooms to Classrooms

A good way to start talking about classroom connections is to consider how one classroom is connected to others, especially when the discussion focuses on the early childhood education classrooms of young children from low-income Latina/o families, who are particularly likely to benefit from a high-functioning and well-integrated system of learning. What is going on in their classrooms is not the only thing that is important, as their classrooms are one part of a much larger schooling environment. The concept of alignment is a useful tool for understanding classroom connections. It might seem less exciting than other early childhood education processes that work directly with kids, but it is absolutely crucial to how those kids are being served. The concept of alignment is itself part of a larger educational philosophy and policy agenda called PK-3. Digging into the issues of alignment and PK-3 and related educational practices is a way of anchoring the educational experiences of young children from low-income Latina/o families at the starting line in something bigger.

Going back to its basic definition, "alignment" refers to the coordination of curriculum, instruction, and activities within and across grades as part of PK-3, which seeks to support a more cohesive educational experience for children transitioning from preschool into the primary grades of elementary school (Bogard & Takanishi, 2005). In terms of policy, alignment is fairly straightforward, involving concrete linkages among standards and practices across classes within any one grade level as well as across contiguous grade levels. Yet, what goes on in the everyday lives of teachers and educators as they actually perceive and execute (or not) alignment is far less clear and too infrequently studied. Consequently, the understanding of how alignment

Claude Bonazzo collaborated with me on this chapter.

actually plays out in the classrooms and hallways of preschools and schools is underdeveloped. That hampers the ability to serve the groups of children often thought to benefit the most from it.

During our time in SWISD, my students and I explored the daily reality of PK-3 instruction for precisely these reasons. We wanted to see how alignment among classrooms worked on the ground to better capture its core elements, identify roadblocks to successful alignment, and determine steps that could be taken to promote alignment. To do so we developed a sense of each classroom on its own, mapped ties among classrooms, and compared classrooms serving different groups of young Latina/o children, distinguished by the representation of students with English language learning needs, in different organizational arrangements, defined by the location of the pre-K program.

In this chapter, I will report what we uncovered about alignment in SWISD by analyzing the large amount of data that my students and I collected through watching and talking. This activity revealed strengths such as alignment among early childhood education classrooms, some visible weaknesses such as less alignment of early childhood education classrooms with classrooms in other grades, and potential methods for balancing out these strengths and weaknesses such as alignment-focused professional development activities.

Alignment within the PK-3 Movement

To begin, I want to return to the widely held view that the expansion of public early childhood education programs is a means of evening out the playing field among children from diverse groups at the starting line and thus a vital tool for districts laboring to meet federal accountability standards (Fuller, 2007). Considerable evidence seems to back up this view, but other evidence seems to undercut it. Specifically, studies have shown that children from historically disadvantaged and disenfranchised groups, including Latina/o children, do demonstrate significant cognitive gains when they enroll in public early childhood education programs. Yet, this evidence is undercut by equally strong evidence of a fade-out of these gains as the primary grades unfold. The students enter elementary school ahead, but their peers without that exposure to public early childhood education programs catch up to them as they move from grade to grade (Duncan & Magnuson, 2013). This vexing fade-out problem has multiple interrelated causes. One likely factor is that children transition from higher-quality early childhood education programs with a great deal of public investment into neglected elementary schools of low quality that cannot sustain the academic momentum from early educational experiences. As succinctly summed up by the developmental psychologist Jeanne Brooks-Gunn (2003, p. 3), "To expect effects to be sustained throughout childhood and adolescence, at their initial high levels, in the absence of continued high quality schooling, however, is to believe in magic." The infusion of resources into early childhood education has not been coupled with equal attention to elementary education, so the durability of those public pre-K efforts is undermined.

PK-3 as a Strategy for Combatting Fade-out

Given the threats of fade-out to the movement to broaden and enrich early childhood experiences, early childhood education advocates have been promoting the PK-3 strategy as a potential remedy to this problem. In the PK-3 strategy, early childhood education, particularly in its public school-based form, is positioned as part of a unified system with the primary grades of elementary school. This systemic approach is intended to facilitate the development of cohesive curricula and learning goals and to foster teacher collaboration within and across units. The motivation behind PK-3 is to invest in and coordinate both sides of the transition into formal schooling so that the targeted children and the public at large get the most out of the large federal and state investments being made in early childhood education in the long term (Bogard & Takanishi, 2005).

Many districts have experimented with the PK-3 model, as the creation of public pre-K programs and the recognition of the value of elementary schools partnering with private early childhood education programs have increased. This model is complex, involving many strategies and activities and requiring the buy-in of multiple institutional actors. Because it involves so much partnership that goes beyond what any one educator is doing in any one classroom, its success rises and falls depending upon the coordination or teamwork of the various stakeholders. Hence, alignment is a real linchpin (Benner et al., 2017; Russakoff, 2011). That crucial element of PK-3 and how it is filled by alignment goes back to the notion of different contexts being in conversation in contextual systems theory.

Alignment as the Key Ingredient

When successful, a PK-3 system is like a smoothly running machine, with many parts operating in synchrony and each part contributing its own necessary components to the overall function. In such a system, alignment is the

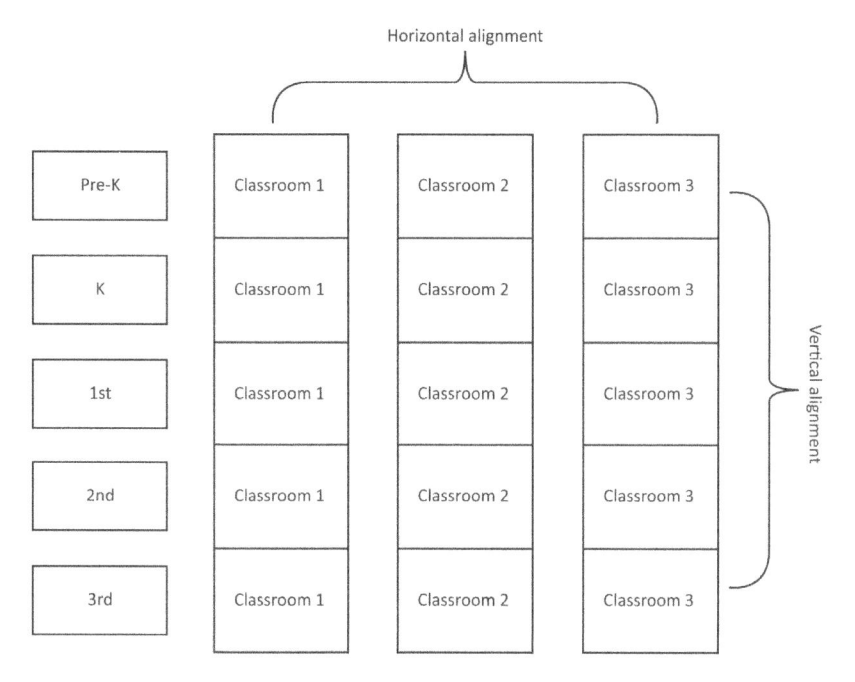

Figure 2.1. Two types of PK–3 alignment in elementary schools

set of practices and norms that link the various pieces of the machinery and coordinate their independent functions into a whole (Kauerz, 2006). Here, that cohesive whole is a seamless transition into and through the primary grades that guards against the fade-out of learning benefits of early childhood education. That is something that children from low-income Latina/o families really need to make the most of the US educational system.

Within this PK-3 machinery, two forms of educational alignment are crucial to understand and implement; they are shown in figure 2.1. Generally, "horizontal alignment" refers to the coordination of instruction, teacher preparation, curricula, programs, and other activities within each individual grade level from the pre-K to third grade. "Vertical alignment" refers to similar coordination, only across rather than within grade levels in this stretch of early education. An example of horizontal alignment might be a group of pre-K teachers in the same school or even spanning a set of schools meeting to coordinate their lesson plans. An example of vertical alignment would be a principal organizing meetings between the school's pre-K teachers and kindergarten teachers to ensure that the curriculum in the latter builds on the curriculum in the former (Kauerz, 2006; Pelletier & Corter, 2006).

Because these concepts are somewhat generic, translating them into more explicit directives for educational practice is important. There are many attempts at such translation. For example, one recommendation from the Foundation for Child Development is that both horizontal and vertical alignment activities should take the forms of principals supporting professional development in within- and across-grade teams of teachers and of teachers regularly participating in professional learning communities that cross classrooms and grades (Kauerz & Coffman, 2013). These working strategies go beyond more abstract conceptualization, but they still do not necessarily speak directly to the everyday experiences of teachers, in how they perceive explicit and implicit alignment activities, what they get from alignment, the challenges to effective alignment that they face, and how they make alignment work in the real world.

Observing Alignment in Action

To achieve an on-the-ground view of alignment in a PK-3 system, I decided that one strategy with potential would be to let concrete and actionable ratings of horizontal and vertical alignment emerge from observations of and discussions with classroom teachers rather than imposing ratings on them. We collected the data through watching and talking and then let that data speak to us about what alignment is in everyday life in classrooms serving young Latina/o children. That approach is called "grounded theory," and it is relevant to both of the major data collection activities we engaged in while at SWISD.

One of these two activities, the semistructured interviews we conducted with the teachers and other school personnel at SWISD, proved to be particularly valuable. These interviews occurred in 36 pre-K classrooms in the 9 SWISD schools we visited and then in 8 kindergarten, 8 first grade, and 6 second grade classrooms that represented the major destinations for children in these pre-K classrooms. Despite our PK-3 focus, we could not extend this data collection into third grade due to the restrictions on time use related to state testing schedules. Importantly, although the interviews covered a lot of ground, alignment received some of the most extensive coverage because the interview guide I designed has several questions about teachers' general orientations to, philosophies about, and experiences with both vertical and horizontal alignment, including the following:

- Do you feel like, as a teacher, you are in it alone, or do you feel part of a larger community of teachers who work together as a team? Who is your community/team?

- How self-contained is your classroom? By that, we mean how much your classroom is linked to other classrooms in the school. What form do these links take?
- Thinking about these concepts of community, team, or links that we have discussed, do they apply more to teachers in the same grade level across schools in SWISD or to the teachers, across grades, in your same school?
- One buzzword in educational policy is "alignment." There is talk of vertical and horizontal alignment. Have you heard of these terms? What do they mean to you?

These interviews with teachers and some aides also covered alignment in a more concrete sense, with respondents asked to discuss their opportunities, especially recent ones at the school or the district level, to coordinate standards and instructional practices with other teachers:

- How often do you and the other teachers in your grade meet? What do you discuss at these meetings?
- Is there a standardized way of leading classes and structuring the day across classrooms in your grade? Are there documents that you can draw on that map out how classrooms are supposed to be run in your grade?
- Do you coordinate with other teachers in the school to make sure that your learning goals match up with the learning goals of the next class your students enter? In other words, do you know if what you are doing in your classroom helps them be ready for the next one, too ready, or not ready enough?

After many interviews with teachers that often lasted a long time, I was somewhat overwhelmed by the amount of data in my reach. To a lesser extent, the portion of the data directly concerning alignment produced a similar surfeit. After transcribing the interviews in either English or Spanish, we set about figuring out how to make sense of all the information. Going into this challenging enterprise, I had some idea of what I might expect, so I and my student Claude explicitly looked for those things. I did not want to be constrained by those a priori ideas, though, so we also looked for new ideas to emerge and allowed ourselves to be led into new possibilities.

Based on what we learned working with these a priori themes and the emergent themes, Claude and I ranked each classroom from pre-K through second grade in terms of both horizontal and vertical alignment and converted those ranks to quantitative rating categories of low, medium, and high alignment. We then organized teacher discussions about actual activities within each alignment category to understand what different levels of alignment look like in actual practice. We also coded teacher discussions of philosophies and challenges to identify common themes within each alignment category that would depict successes and challenges in translating theory into reality.

Most of the activity involved in the exploration of alignment leveraged the interview data from SWISD, the talking part of our time there, but we supplemented this activity with the watching part based on the CLASS, a standardized protocol for observing and rating the quality of classroom activities and interactions (Pianta, La Paro, & Hamre, 2007). My students and I conducted the CLASS in all 58 pre-K, kindergarten, first grade, and second grade classrooms. In all of these classrooms spanning early childhood education into the primary grades of elementary school, we eventually had seven-point ratings (low to high) of classroom organization, instructional support, and emotional support (table I.1). After organizing and analyzing the interview data, the CLASS data shed light on how PK-3 alignment issues mapped onto more general dimensions of classroom quality within and across schools and grade levels.

This exploration of alignment at SWISD also took advantage of the district's interesting experiment in where to place pre-K classrooms. In SWISD, public pre-K is embedded within elementary schools across the city, but some elementary schools did not have the physical capacity to devote classroom space to pre-K. Consequently, the district reopened a former elementary school as a pre-K campus to serve all pre-K classrooms for six elementary schools. At the Cole Pre-K Campus, pre-K teachers worked side by side in the same building, even when they were technically employed by different elementary schools. That arrangement, I believed, could give special insight into alignment. At Cole, pre-K teachers were at a remove from other teachers in their schools but closely connected with pre-K teachers from other schools. Outside of Cole, pre-K teachers were in closer proximity to primary grade teachers and to each other but at a remove from other pre-K teachers in the district. Consequently, our sample of classrooms included all pre-K classrooms at Cole, K-2 classrooms in two schools with their pre-K programs housed at Cole, and K-2 classrooms in seven schools with their pre-K programs on their own grounds.

Thus, during my time at SWISD, I looked into how alignment worked, whether alignment worked differently depending on the extent to which classrooms were populated by young Latina/o children from low-income families and whether classrooms were situated in elementary school or pre-K campus settings.

The Elusiveness of Alignment

We based our approach for identifying low, medium, and high alignment, both vertical and horizontal, on the classroom, not the school. We used what we observed at SWISD to assess the degree to which any one classroom exhibited evidence of being aligned with other classrooms in its grade (horizontal) and/or with classrooms across grades (vertical). Doing so allowed us to see that no matter how uniform policies and standards might be, alignment activities are likely to vary from classroom to classroom and from teacher to teacher. I could, however, aggregate alignment ratings within schools to compare how consistent alignment looks across classrooms in one school versus another.

A General Picture of Alignment

The bottom-line conclusion from this process is that only a tiny number of pre-K, kindergarten, first grade, and second grade classrooms at SWISD could be characterized as high in alignment; high levels of vertical alignment were even rarer. Notably, the few classrooms that looked better in terms of alignment also typically scored quite well on the various quality ratings of the CLASS, suggesting that alignment is likely a sign of good classrooms more generally. Overall, even the classrooms that were connected to the most observable alignment activities only loosely reflected, at best, broad recommendations in the educational research literature about alignment, such as creating leadership teams to pursue alignment activities under a concrete strategic plan (Kauerz & Coffman, 2013).

Consequently, a better way to differentiate among the classrooms at SWISD was to separate classrooms with no clear evidence of alignment activities from those that had some evidence of alignment activities. I fully recognize that this bar is low, but it does represent the reality of alignment in the daily goings-on of schools regardless of what the official policy or practice of the school or district is. Figure 2.2 presents a breakdown of the SWISD classrooms in our study in terms of horizontal and vertical alignment.

The good news is that very few classrooms exhibited no or minimal evidence of either kind of alignment, and the majority of classrooms exhibited non-negligible evidence of both. The bad news is that for a near minority of classrooms, evidence of horizontal alignment did not go along with evidence of vertical alignment. In those classrooms, which made up over one-third of the sample of SWISD classrooms, efforts were being made to align classrooms within grade levels (horizontal) but not across grade levels (ver-

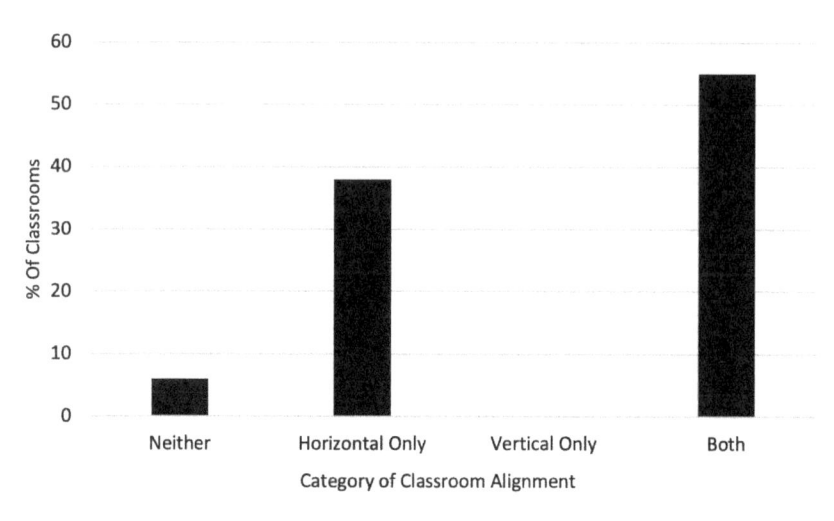

Figure 2.2. Proportion of classrooms in various alignment categories

tical). Thus, experiences within a grade were somewhat similar and coordinated, but a multigrade sequence of coordinated classrooms was harder to find.

Differences in Alignment Related to School Arrangement

The general trend in PK-3 alignment in SWISD schools was a bit disappointing. Still, this general breakdown of alignment differed in potentially telling ways according to how pre-K classrooms were connected to their destination classrooms in the primary grades of their schools. About 40 percent of the classrooms in the sample were connected to the Cole Pre-K Campus, meaning that they were pre-K classrooms housed at Cole or they were K-2 classrooms in schools that housed their pre-K classrooms at Cole.

All instances of classrooms showing no evidence of horizontal or vertical alignment were in the Cole feeder system; they were Cole classrooms or destinations of Cole classrooms. Moreover, the majority of classrooms in or connected to Cole demonstrated evidence of horizontal alignment only; they constituted most of the classrooms in the sample that fell into the horizontal-only category (figure 2.3).

In the early childhood and primary grade classrooms outside of the Cole feeder pattern, that is, pre-K classrooms on the physical sites of their destination elementary schools and the K-2 classrooms into which those pre-K classrooms fed, nearly three-fourths demonstrated evidence of both horizontal and vertical alignment. In these same classrooms, horizontal-only alignment was much rarer. Finally, none of the non-Cole classrooms fell into the neither horizontal nor vertical category.

Thus, the Cole campus arrangement in SWISD, which separated pre-K classrooms from their contiguous primary grades to group pre-K classrooms together across schools, appeared to foster horizontal alignment among pre-K classrooms quite well. That apparent benefit of the Cole arrangement, however, seemed to come at the expense of developing vertical alignment between pre-K and the primary grades.

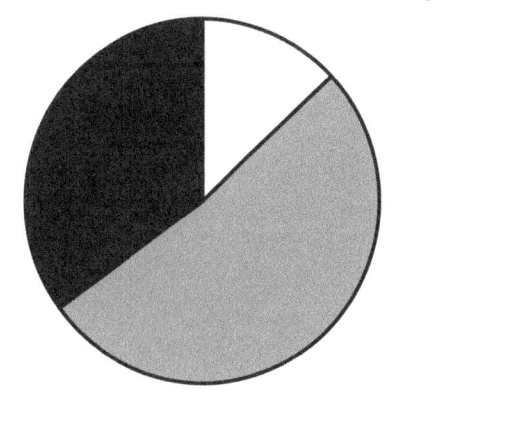

Classrooms Connected to the Pre-K Campus

☐ Neither
▨ Horizontal Only
■ Both

Classrooms Not Connected to the Pre-K Campus

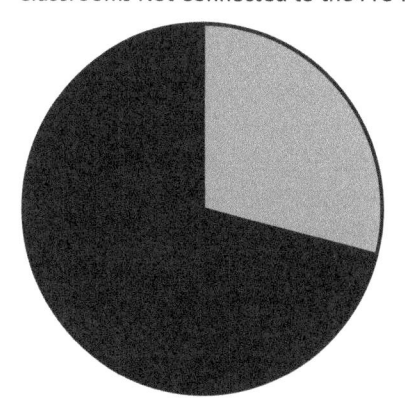

Figure 2.3. Breakdown of alignment categories, by site of pre-K classrooms

Differences in Alignment Related to Student Composition

The general picture of alignment we saw also differed according to the language instruction status of the classrooms. Most of the classrooms we studied at SWISD served largely low-income Latina/o populations, but they also revealed the heterogeneity of the population of young Latina/o children from low-income families. Classroom language status identifies diverse segments of that population according to families' language use, which in turn directly reflects families' migration histories from Latin America and indirectly their socioeconomic circumstances.

Two-thirds of the classrooms that I and my students visited could be designated, officially by the district or not, as having bilingual instruction. A few of these classrooms in the primary grades had a dual-language instruction format, meaning that they mixed English language learners with other children and switched back and forth between Spanish and English languages in instruction. Those dual-language instruction classrooms are designed to expose children, regardless of their backgrounds or their home languages, to learning activities in different languages. The belief is that doing so will help them develop the cognitive benefits of being multilingual.

The overwhelming majority of the bilingual classrooms, however, were populated by English language learners and focused on developing English skills while also covering academic content in Spanish and English. Those types of bilingual classrooms are more in line with common perceptions of "English as second language" education for children from immigrant families. For the most part, classrooms in this latter category, traditional bilingual instruction that is not dual-language instruction, became less common as grade level increased within and across schools. At the pre-K level, more than 70 percent of classrooms in and out of the Cole Pre-K Campus had bilingual instruction but without the dual-language format. This proportion fell to the 50–60 percent range in the primary grades, again inside and outside the Cole feeder pattern. I label such classrooms as being primarily Spanish-speaking or, more simply, primarily Spanish, because in everyday practice, they featured little English instruction.

As figure 2.4 shows, fewer than 40 percent of bilingual (primarily Spanish-speaking) classrooms demonstrated evidence of both horizontal and vertical alignment. Turning to the other classrooms, nearly 80 percent of the classrooms with English-only instruction demonstrated both alignments, and the classrooms with dual-language instructional formats, which featured a greater balance of Spanish and English, were more similar to the monolingual classrooms than to the other supposedly bilingual classrooms.

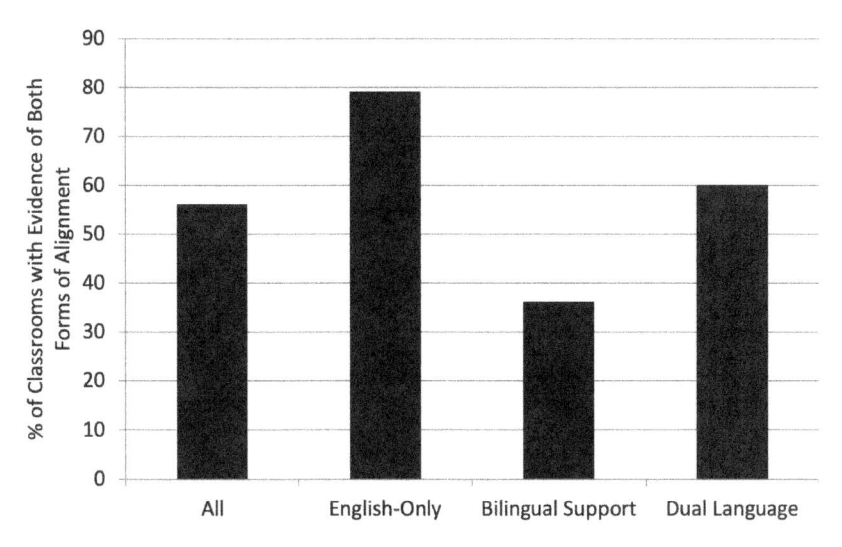

Figure 2.4. Breakdown of classrooms with two types of alignment, by language instruction status

Thus, if horizontal and vertical alignments support the instruction and learning of children in disadvantaged circumstances, then one such group of young Latina/o children—English language learners—appears to be less likely to have that support at SWISD. They face more obstacles to success in the US educational system, so they could be especially affected by that missing support.

How Alignment Works

Overall and across all types of pre-K classrooms and the kindergarten, first grade, and second grade classrooms they fed into in SWISD, horizontal alignment was more common than vertical alignment. Still, there were both similarities and differences in how each of these two types of alignment worked when they were in action.

How Horizontal Alignment Works

Typically, teachers within a grade level at a school met at least briefly on a weekly basis to review themes, assessments, standards, and curricula. These activities certainly reflected strong administrative suggestion and even administrative mandate; their supervisors encouraged the meetings or made teachers meet. What I want to stress, though, is that they also reflected general teacher customs, which is perhaps even more important. Such regular face-to-face interactions among teachers were the norm within grades if not across grades.

In our assessment during our time in SWISD, one elementary school with an on-site pre-K program provided the clearest example of effective horizontal alignment in action. Indeed, this particular school was one of the few in which horizontal alignment could be considered high and in which it was seen as connecting same-grade classrooms across schools and not just within the school. This school, Chavez Elementary,[1] was predominantly Latina/o and located in the poor eastern side of the city. During the school year of our study, it received a state school accountability rating of "Recognized" and a district accountability rating of "Academically Acceptable."

In the view of teachers, the cornerstone of alignment at Chavez was the strong sense of community that had developed among the teaching staff and administrators over the years and had become akin to a family atmosphere. A pre-K teacher in the school, Ms. Leon, said, "That's why I love it, 'cause if something's wrong with you or somebody else and they need your help, somebody is always there, not only with the grade level but other teachers and the administration." A certified bilingual pre-K teacher with 32 years of experience including 14 at Chavez and 8 in early childhood education, Ms. Leon believed that this community spirit filtered down into professional activities, facilitating alignment within grades. Connections fostered talk, which facilitated horizontal alignment.

All pre-K teachers at Chavez met at least once a week and sometimes more to coordinate activities and plan lessons for the following week. They were guided by state guidelines for pre-K core curricula, but they had flexibility in what they did within that curriculum and took advantage of it. They tried to be consistent among themselves in what they were doing in their classrooms. Importantly, they had all participated in the same state-sponsored professional development program for pre-K teachers, which consisted of a series of online and in-person courses aiming to facilitate teachers' understanding and use of research-based instructional practices; I refer to that program here as First Step. Ms. Leon emphasized how the program helped the pre-K teachers meet standards by working together as a team from a shared base. She said, "The kids, it's like five or six years ago, what I'm doing now I would never think that [with] these kids it could hap-

---

1. All schools and teachers have been given pseudonyms in this book. SWISD is the same pseudonym used in Crosnoe et al. 2015.

pen, but it can. And with [First Step], it really does help the kids learn their letters and sounds and rhyming words because there are games that we can do with them."

At least in part, Ms. Leon attributed her teaching success in early childhood education to her engagement with this professional development program. Why this engagement matters to the issue of horizontal alignment is that all the pre-K teachers agreed to engage in it. That shared engagement helped to ensure that the various pre-K classrooms at Chavez had a united front in daily activities and overall goals. That this program came from the state level down and was encouraged by the district also increased the alignment of pre-K classrooms at Chavez with pre-K classrooms more broadly across the district and state, including those serving Latina/o children from low-income families and those serving other demographic and socioeconomic groups of young children.

Ms. Leon and her fellow teachers did not believe that their teaching activities were being dictated to them or that their classrooms were being standardized. Instead, they believed that they were receiving help with their teaching that could be shared widely. They did not see alignment as an end itself but rather as a means of ensuring that any one classroom out of many was a good place for children, particularly young Latina/o children, to learn. The teachers saw horizontal alignment as a way of getting it right at the starting line.

How Vertical Alignment Works

Although interaction, consultation, and coordination among teachers in the same grade have had a long history in US schools, the connections across grade levels, including contiguous ones, have been far less common. In many ways, each grade can exist in its own bubble, near but disconnected from others even as students move from one level to the next. Consequently, efforts to achieve vertical alignment face a greater uphill battle than efforts to achieve horizontal alignment. Vertical alignment can be a hassle, and it goes against the norm.

Fewer classrooms demonstrated evidence of vertical alignment than evidence of horizontal alignment, but the majority of classrooms we observed did have some form of vertical alignment. Valleybrook is one elementary school with an on-site early childhood education program in SWISD that could be characterized as having high levels of vertical alignment. It is a socioeconomically diverse school in the center of the district with large numbers of Latina/o English language learners but also a popular dual-language program. It was labeled "Recognized" and "Academically Acceptable" in the state and district school accountability rating systems.

Valleybrook is one of the smallest schools in our sample, and many of the teachers there said its small size facilitated more cross-grade interaction. The entire teaching staff met as a group, but actual planning meetings typically took place in smaller clusters of grades. Pre-K, kindergarten, and first grade constituted one such cluster. Vertical alignment was clearly on the minds of the teachers, especially among the pre-K teachers. They tended to define their success in terms of how well their students would be prepared to take on the tasks of kindergarten, which meant that they oriented their teaching to what the kindergarten teachers were doing at the same time and therefore to what their students would probably be doing the following year when they entered kindergarten. As a result, the pre-K and kindergarten teachers were particularly focused on achieving some alignment between the two grade levels within Valleybrook. A pre-K teacher at the school said her idea of community encompassed the other pre-K teachers and all the kindergarten teachers.

Ms. Frances, a fourth-year pre-K teacher with certification in early childhood education and English as a second language instruction, was quite explicit about the need for vertical alignment in schools with early childhood education programs. She said that, in general, vertical alignment involved teams working together to connect elementary, middle, and high schools but that in practice, vertical alignment worked in smaller units. Within those smaller units, regular interactions among teachers in contiguous grades over the year allowed teachers to better understand the expectations their students would face in the following grade and the preparation their students would likely have before entering their own grade. She recognized that this integration was facilitated by the learning standards mapped out by the district and supported through district-level training programs. On the school level, Valleybrook's organization of cross-grade meetings over the course of the year helped to maintain the momentum behind alignment. Ms. Frances told us,

> We would all be off of work for a day and have like a planning day type of thing. But we meet at faculty meetings similar to that and committees similar to that. But probably at least two times a year we really make sure that we're kind of on the same page, that we're getting those things done. If not, we [ask], "How do you think we can start accomplishing this before the end of the year?"

Tellingly, every pre-K, kindergarten, and first grade classroom at Valleybrook was rated as showing some evidence of vertical alignment across classrooms. Moreover, the evidence for vertical alignment was often considerably more than the average in the full sample of classrooms in the district. The second grade classrooms, which were not as actively involved in the early grade activity meetings, were not rated as vertically aligned. Thus, the small school setting likely was a contributing factor in the vertical alignment at Valleybrook but only in the earliest grades whose teachers viewed themselves and were defined by the school as part of the team or community.

A Special Case

The Cole Pre-K Campus is a unique feature of SWISD. It is also something of an outlier in terms of alignment within the district. The clear throughline of my time in SWISD is that the Cole set-up seemed to foster horizontal alignment but not to foster and maybe even to disrupt vertical alignment.

As a pre-K campus, Cole had an unusually large number of pre-K classrooms, more than all the classrooms across grades in Valleybrook. Cole classrooms were divided into six color-coded teams. The team teachers met every week to plan the content coverage and instructional themes for the next week. The degree to which these planning sessions involved the learning objectives and activities of kindergarten varied by teams, often for idiosyncratic reasons. That is why some classrooms at Cole demonstrated evidence of both vertical alignment and horizontal alignment rather than horizontal alignment alone. What helped make these planning sessions work and what made them easy to organize was that all the teachers involved were dedicated to and trained in early childhood education. Moreover, they all engaged in the same professional development programs. As a result, they were working from the same basic model of classroom instruction; they spoke the same professional language and had a shared understanding of goals.

Some teachers at Cole defined a good classroom as one that is team-oriented, so the spirit of alignment is in the air. They generally discussed their community in terms of their team members but also more broadly as all teachers and administrators at Cole. One thing that was not lost on me was that they rarely mentioned the other teachers in their home elementary schools.

Ms. Ortiz was a certified teacher at Cole who had earned a master's degree in education and had 10 years of teaching experience, including seven years in early childhood education. She explained how she and her fellow team members at Cole created links and activities about once every week or two that ranged from watching videos to doing science experiments. She went on to say,

> We do a lot of activities with about three other classrooms, so that's where the whole thing [comes in] that I was just talking about, kind of intermingling with other teachers to bounce ideas and stuff off each other. So we try to, at least I try to and ... about three or four other teachers try to either switch students or integrate our classes together and do an activity together and things like that.

The weekly meetings were also supplemented by other series of focus meetings throughout the year that covered more specific topics. The groups at these meetings acted as teams within teams, such as for science, oral literacy, and gross motor skills, and often had their own special nights for particular functions that involved parents. From Ms. Ortiz we got a picture of a campus in constant communication about content, planning, and materials that crisscrossed various units and connected them. The state and district guidelines for pre-K as well as the First Step professional development program provided some structure to this communication, but it was also organic.

Although Cole did not provide the best example of vertical alignment in SWISD, it did offer an important lesson about vertical alignment. The classrooms that were rated as showing some evidence of vertical alignment were generally led by teachers who had experience in other grades before taking jobs in pre-K. That means the working memory teachers develop over their careers about what is expected and supported across multiple grade levels through their own experiences in different grades can facilitate vertical alignment. Such alignment is more individual in that it is not necessarily fostered through interaction but on a more personal basis.

Ms. Garza, a bilingual teacher, drew on her past as an elementary schoolteacher and the connections she maintained with former colleagues in other grades when she approached teaching in pre-K. She had been teaching for 18 years, mostly in kindergarten, first, second, and fourth grades. Like many teachers with such a history, she said schools could only be successful when teachers learned from each other and asked each other for help. Yet, in addition to asking others for help, she also derived help and guidance in the present classroom from her past classrooms. In a sense, this teacher was acting as her own channel of vertical alignment, and her sense of the value of vertical alignment is what actually led her into pre-K in the first place, as she explained:

Because I've taught the other grades, I know what's coming up for them, so I can push them a little further along, which is one of the reasons why I went to the other grades. So I wanted to know what was going on over there, and really all I found [was] it's pretty much the same thing. It's just higher vocabulary in a little greater depth but the same. And so I came back down here because I found when I was in fourth grade, some of those kids couldn't read at the second grade level. Some [who recently arrived in the United States] hadn't been to school in Mexico, and that was really hard for them. So they get into being identified as . . . special ed, and they, really, they're not. They just haven't been to school. So I came back down because I knew that if the foundations aren't there, then you're not going to be able to build anything.

Throughout the teams at Cole, teachers like Ms. Garza used the district's curricular road maps to guide them in what students needed to know. They also drew on the provided assessments and rubrics to gauge how ready those students were for kindergarten. The teachers then worked together to find ways to achieve their goals within this organizational structure. They were connected to each other, but they were also sometimes closed off from teachers in grades their classes fed into, unless the teachers themselves had been in those classrooms.

Perceived Challenges to Alignment

All the teachers whom we observed and interviewed in SWISD were aware of and endorsed the basic concept of alignment in both its horizontal and vertical forms. They agreed that alignment was important in theory, but they also had problems translating that theory into reality as they went through their daily activities at school. Those challenges are important to consider.

Practical Barriers

One major challenge was specific to the organizational structure of the Cole Pre-K Campus. In this structure, pre-K students started and ended the day at their elementary schools but were bused to Cole for their actual classroom time. Separated from their partner teachers in primary grades, pre-K teachers at Cole relied mostly on guidelines, road maps, and rubrics to stay vertically aligned, but the lack of easy communication across grade levels that were physically separated was a barrier to a more interactional form of vertical alignment. Pre-K teachers at Cole rarely received any feedback from the other campuses about how their students were doing when they entered elementary school or what they might need to improve upon to help their students better prepare for elementary school. One teacher at Cole described how someone would receive feedback from the principal at their official elementary school: "Only if there's a big problem, but like it would be great if you could, you know, if you got a report 'Oh, your kids …' Even though I hear that some principals go around saying, 'Can you make a list of the kids that are doing great and who taught them at [Cole]?' I hear that that happens a little bit."

If the many teachers on the enormous Cole Pre-K Campus were not getting any feedback from the elementary schools where their students would soon be attending as kindergartners, how could they make sure they and their pre-K classrooms were aligned with the teachers and classrooms of that specific elementary school? This issue was indeed compounded by the busing arrangement that kept pre-K teachers from having regular contact with their students' parents. The lack of regular contact between teachers and parents is important, considering that parental involvement in education is viewed as a vital support for PK-3 alignment.

The Isolation of Early Childhood Educators

Although the physical separation between pre-K and primary grades only occurred at the Cole Pre-K Campus and its feeder schools, all the schools we studied in SWISD evidenced something akin to psychic separation. By that I mean the pre-K teachers in every single school in the sample voiced concerns that they were not fully vertically aligned with activities in their elementary schools or that they were not viewed as equal partners by their fellow teachers. Pre-K teachers were more concerned about their participation in vertical alignment with the primary grades than primary grade teachers were about aligning with pre-K. A teacher at Chavez explained with a laugh, "[In] pre-K … we walk, walk alone, and sometimes we're like the stepchild that's not … we're not even at the table, but if they'll throw us the food we're pretty happy."

In other words, kindergarten, first grade, and second grade teachers in the SWISD schools we studied were more likely to say pre-K was part of the elementary school than were the pre-K teachers themselves. This pattern is both a product of a lack of vertical alignment in elementary schools with early childhood education programs and also a source of that insufficient alignment.

The Big-School Problem

Another apparent challenge to alignment was school size. Larger schools with more pre-K classes seemed to be less vertically aligned than smaller schools with only a handful of pre-K classrooms. Schools with large early childhood education programs often evidenced significant horizontal alignment, including at the Cole Pre-K Campus.

In smaller schools like Valleybrook, teachers were more connected to each other and able to share information with teachers from other grades in formal settings such as schoolwide meetings and in less formal ways such as during lunch or recess. A pre-K teacher explained how teachers often interacted at Scott, a small socioeconomically and racially/ethnically diverse school in an affluent section of the central part of the city: "A lot of it is in passing or after school if we see, we typically stop into each other's rooms and see what's going on. We do check in regularly with each other. And is it a formal meeting? No. It's just more like, 'Hey, I'm doing this or this is what I'm doing.' So, yeah . . . at least a couple times out of the week I stop in and talk with them."

From Challenges to Strategies

Although the challenges to alignment, especially vertical alignment, in elementary schools with early childhood education programs are significant, the teachers we talked with also noted several strategies they used to stay connected to other teachers. These strategies might be considered "self-alignment." Self-alignment appeared to be especially important to vertical alignment.

Many teachers said the best way they could achieve vertical alignment was to maintain a good sense of the standards for teaching and learning for contiguous grade levels; a kindergarten teacher would stay abreast of the standards for pre-K and first grade apart from discussions with teachers in those grades. Certain professional developmental activities used by the district, such as the First Step program, facilitated this cross-grade awareness.

Many veteran teachers had taught multiple grades over the years and used their experience to vertically align their classrooms with what was going on across grades. Ms. Ortiz at Cole explained that her time teaching kindergarten and first grade was a support for alignment: "I know what they need to go into. . . . I guess me teaching kinder[garten], I kind of have an advantage because I know what they're going into kinder expecting them to know."

Moving Forward

"Alignment" is a good example of a term from educational policy and practice that is widely recognized but insufficiently understood. Alignment is clearly important to the success of PK-3 initiatives as a strategy for reducing the fade-out effects of early childhood education among young Latina/o children from low-income families. Far less is known about how alignment actually works when teachers come to school every day. Our time on the ground in SWISD, a school district at the demographic frontier of the United States as well as a site of major and often innovative public pre-K activity, revealed that alignment is valued by teachers and prioritized by them and their administrations but also that it is difficult to pull off consistently. The policies were there, but the daily activities did not always follow them.

Clearly, horizontal alignment is more readily doable than vertical alignment. It builds on long-standing customs of within-grade coordination, capitalizes on existing relationships, and reflects how most schools are organized. Getting teachers to work across grade levels seems to be more challenging, even if they endorse doing so. This obstacle to vertical alignment is made more significant when pre-K classrooms are involved, as they are still too often viewed as outside the traditional structures of elementary schools. The pre-K teachers we interviewed saw themselves as being at a remove from their schools and the other teachers in them. Regardless of whether these perceptions were accurate, they likely affected what teachers were doing. One take-away lesson from our time at SWISD was that both horizontal and vertical alignment grew out of a sense of community; in itself it did not build a sense of community. Given the traditional grade-specific structures of elementary schools, grade-level teachers might have a head start on building that sense of community, which then facilitates their alignment. Efforts to build a sense of community across grades, therefore, would be needed to make up the difference between horizontal and vertical alignment.

Two special cases in SWISD are worth highlighting. The first is that the Cole Pre-K Campus is an example of an innovative educational strategy that has an upside and a downside. Having so many pre-K teachers together in one building without any competition with other grades certainly fostered a sense of partnership that manifested in many horizontal alignment activities. Yet these same supports for horizontal alignment were barriers to vertical alignment. The degree to which the loss of vertical alignment was countered by the gain in horizontal alignment in the effectiveness of instruction at Cole is hard to determine, but it needs to be examined. The many advantages Cole offered teachers and students would be more fully realized if the vertical alignment issue could be resolved.

The second case is that the early childhood education and primary grade classrooms that were populated by the most English language learners—almost always young Latina/o children from low-income families—tended to be lower in alignment activities. This pattern is likely related to the more general challenges posed by such classrooms (Goldenberg, 2008). Given that the task of facilitating English on top of regular content instruction can be difficult to manage, teachers may struggle to act on many of their best intentions, such as following through on alignment activities.

Overall, the results of this exploration suggest that the measurement of alignment in larger-scale quantitative studies of the early childhood education of young Latina/o children by researchers and evaluations of actual organizational processes in early childhood education programs and schools serving this population should prioritize assessing the following elements:

- the existence of school policies for promoting alignment such as required meetings and creation of teams within and across grades,
- the number of such alignment activities in which teachers actually participate,
- the efforts teachers make to be aware of standards in contiguous grade levels, and
- the degree to which teachers feel a sense of community in their schools both within and across grades.

Theoretically, alignment should be viewed as the product of three interacting forces: the personal and professional motivation to align such as how much it is valued and mandated; barriers to acting on that motivation in the form of distance, physical or psychic, and practical constraints such as time; and organizational and social supports for overcoming these barriers in the form of professional development, interpersonal connections, and so forth. Translating that theory into reality is a step toward better addressing the current educational needs and promoting the future educational prospects of young Latina/o children from low-income families at the starting line.

CHAPTER 3

Connecting Families, Schools, and Communities

Another way to contextually connect the early childhood education of young children from low-income Latina/o families is to consider exchanges among the three primary contexts of their young lives: early childhood education classrooms, families, and communities. Children from all walks of life, including Latina/o children, go back and forth between home and school, both of which are embedded in communities. The convergence of these three contexts matters, not just each on its own, but that convergence can take many forms, both positive and negative. Following contextual systems theory, I tend to prioritize convergence that looks like all sides are in conversation, talking with and listening to each other and doing both consistently.

That conversation is at the heart of the concept of family-school-community partnerships. This concept emphasizes that children learn the most and best live up to their potential when there is a coordinated set of values, standards, practices, and expectations among the adults and adult institutions in their lives that is built gradually and purposefully over time (Epstein, 2018). Increasingly, building such partnerships and encouraging that conversation have been the focus of policy and practice, from initiatives within specific schools to large-scale federal policies such as No Child Left Behind. Yet, getting these three contexts in conversation with each other and helping them become partners is easier said than done. That goal takes time and effort, and the three sides genuinely have to know each other. Often, the various sides think that they are in conversation even when they are not; they are talking to but not with each other, and one side is dominating the supposed conversation. The assumptions that underlie the dis-

---

Claude Bonazzo collaborated with me on this chapter and engaged with similar ideas and data in his dissertation research, which grew out of this project.

cussion and interaction remain below the surface and keep them from truly coming together. The challenges to staying in conversation may be especially acute for the population of low-income Latina/o parents with young children entering school. There are often language barriers keeping families and communities on one side and schools on the other, and the lack of long-term familiarity with the US educational system in immigrant families and communities may lead to parents, communities, and educators talking past each other even when they do talk.

For these reasons I have long been interested in family-school-community partnerships in general and specifically those involving Latina/o Americans, particularly immigrants. These issues have driven a good deal of my research as a sociologist focused on families, schools, and children, which is why I went into my time at SWISD ready to identify situations in which families, schools, and communities were on the same page and to understand why they were. I was equally interested in identifying situations in which they were not on the same page and understanding why not. This chapter gets into what I, with the help of my student Claude, found in the process. The long and short of it is that at the starting line, early childhood educators and low-income Latina/o parents overwhelmingly value family-school-community partnerships, often have trouble living up to those values, and have even more trouble discerning when and how they are not.

Bringing Families, Schools, and Communities Together

Regarding alignment among classrooms in the PK-3 system, there tends to be an underlying sentiment in research and policy on alignment that places the central foci on the early childhood education classrooms. From that perspective, alignment joins all sides, but the focus is more on one side than the others. Historically, something similar has happened in the world of research and policy on family-school-community partnerships; it has tended to focus more on what families are doing than the other two actors in the partnership. That focus rightly recognizes the absolutely crucial role of parents in children's lives. Yet, it also places a heavy burden on parents in ways that may be unfair or that do not always recognize inequalities that stratify parents' opportunities to get their children ahead or have their voices heard. Thus, I want to start this discussion of family-school-community partnerships by discussing parents and their relations with the educational system.

Early Focus on Parents' Involvement

Policy makers, educators, and parents have long understood that children are more likely to succeed academically when the parents are actively engaged in their educational careers. That is why the concept of parental involvement in education has been the focus of so much research among educational scholars. A good definition of parental involvement in education is the package of behaviors and attitudes that parents develop and use to support and manage their children's educational experiences and schooling pursuits (Crosnoe, 2012). This definition is generally discussed in terms of parents' behaviors and attitudes in three domains that I can describe with an explicit focus on how parents get and stay involved in the education of young children (Epstein, 2018; Ginsburg et al., 2010; Hoover-Dempsey & Sandler, 1997; Pomerantz et al., 2007; Reynolds & Shlafer, 2010).

Parents can be involved at home by constructing cognitively stimulating environments that encourage and support children's learning and skill development. They might provide books and other learning materials; engage children in learning activities such as reading, puzzles, and games; talk up the value of education; and maintain a steady stream of talk and conversation that exposes children to complex language. Parents can be involved in preschool or school settings by consistently interacting with and talking with teachers about children and their educational needs and goals, participating in school activities, connecting with other parents, and understanding and reinforcing what children are doing in the classroom. Parents can be involved in the broader communities where they live and where schools are typically located by exposing them to stimulating and engaging programs, events, and public institutions such as art classes, museum exhibits, and libraries. Families can build social networks with other residents to expand their access to important information about educational opportunities and services.

These kinds of parental involvement behaviors have been studied extensively by social and behavioral scientists over many decades, with special attention to how they are associated with common indicators of children's academic performance. For the most part, this research has shown that these associations do exist in expected positive directions. Indeed, reviews of the parental involvement literature covering the K-12 years and early childhood education have reported that the link between parents' involvement behaviors that are well-suited to their children's ages and stages of education on one hand and academic performance on the other is quite consistent across a range of studies (Pomerantz et al., 2007; Reynolds & Shlafer, 2010). Dimensions of academic performance linked to parental involvement include school assessments, test scores, academic attitudes, and social behavior.

Why might parental involvement in education work as an academic booster for children? One reason for these statistical associations in studies undoubtedly has nothing to do with the potential for parental involvement to work. That is because some portion of these associations reflect "reverse causality"; that is, parental involvement in education does not lead to better academic outcomes so much as more academically successful children invite more educational involvement from parents. The associations also may reflect "spuriousness"; some other factor such as higher parental education is simultaneously leading parents to be more educationally involved and increasing children's achievement. Thus, parental involvement appears to be an academic boost, but some of that appearance is a mirage. Of the portion of these associations that is real, however, the most commonly discussed reasons parental involvement in education might really matter include the messages that parents' behaviors are sending to their children about the value of education, the stimulation of cognitive development afforded by parentally constructed learning activities, the practical utility of the knowledge and information gained by parents about the educational system through school activities and community networks, the coordinated teamwork of parents and educators to best serve children's interests and needs, and the ways parental engagement signifies to schools that children are worthy of investment (Cheadle, 2008; Hill, 2001; Hoover-Dempsey & Sandler, 1997; Lareau, 2003; Pomerantz et al., 2007; Raver et al., 2007).

The idea that parental involvement is an educational resource that matters more for those with less access to educational resources overall has long held sway in both research and policy. An actively involved parent may be important for children whose academic pursuits are also supported by money to fund outside-of-school activities and supports such as math camps and tutoring and by family social status that decreases the likelihood that a child's special needs will be ignored; for example, the parents might demand help with learning difficulties or investment in apparent talents. The importance of those parents' involvement, however, overlaps with what their children are getting from these other resources, so that the supports are sometimes redundant. For children without those other resources, parental involvement in education becomes the most important or only support. As a result, the link between parental involvement and children's schooling outcomes should be greater for children from more disadvantaged or disenfranchised families and communities than it is for children from families and communities with more money, influence, and power. That is why policy and programs to improve the academic fortunes of children from low-income, racial/ethnic minority, and/or immigrant backgrounds have so often emphasized getting parents involved in schools. This same idea is why such efforts have become particularly popular and visible when targeting children from low-income Latina/o families, both young children (Crosnoe, 2012) and older children (Hill & Tyson, 2009).

Challenges to Parental Involvement Efforts

Parental involvement in education would seem to be a good thing, and it certainly does matter greatly to the academic prospects of children from disadvantaged and disenfranchised families and communities and for the academic performance of their schools. At the same time, the focus of research and policy on parental involvement in education has generated significant critiques over the years, particularly about the magnitude and meaning of its effects on children, the failure to identify explanatory mechanisms for any effects that are strong and real, and whether traditional conceptions of parental involvement in education are culturally biased. At least partially reflecting the value of these critiques, policy and programmatic efforts to leverage parental involvement in education for academic gains in such families and communities do not always work (Domina, 2005; Robinson & Harris, 2014).

One important critique that warrants attention is that the whole notion of parental involvement in education is one-sided. It is all about parents and parental behavior rather than about the various actors in a children's education and the ongoing interactions among them. Parents in two families may engage in the exact same involvement behaviors to different effects because schools are differentially aware of and receptive to these behaviors. School personnel may know that one parent is scaffolding learning at school with activities at home and invest in the child as a result while not investing in another parent's child at school simply because they do not know how engaged that parent is with the child at home. As another example, two parents may have the same motivation to be involved at school, but the school invites, welcomes, and affirms one parent's involvement attempts but not the other's involvement attempts. Viewing parental involvement as solely within the parent, therefore, is naïve and misguided. Understanding the limitations of that view is especially important in the case of parents from disadvantaged or disenfranchised populations. Vis-à-vis their children's preschools and schools, they are less likely to have their involvement behaviors elicited or rewarded and more likely to have their involvement behaviors misinterpreted or ignored (Adair & Tobin, 2008; Bryk & Schneider, 2003; Lareau, 2003; McWayne et al., 2013; Robinson & Harris, 2014).

Thus, parental involvement in education is a potential resource for supporting the educational futures of young children, but that potential is not often fully realized because it is too narrowly and too simplistically considered. My own research has shown that these issues are quite acute for low-income and often immigrant Latina/o families.

Emphasizing Partnerships

As the limitations of focusing on parental involvement in education in a one-sided, decontextualized way have become clearer, there has been a push in research and policy to approach it as part of an exchange. To go back to contextual systems theory, parental involvement is one direction in a bidirectional transaction. The idea is that parents are one element of a relationship between family and school, family and community, and community and school, with children in the middle rather than an isolated element of a person or an institution (Christenson & Sheridan, 2001). Again, this shift toward a contextual systems view has been particularly valuable for understanding and serving young children from historically disadvantaged and disenfranchised populations.

One-Sided to Multisided

If parental involvement in education is one-sided, family-school-community partnerships come into play as conduits of multisided transactions. The word "partnership" implies that the different contexts consistently work together and coordinate in the best interests of the children. That coordination reinforces what is going on in any one context and reduces the odds that any two contexts are at cross-purposes, undermine each other, or overlap to the point of redundancy. Partnerships are characterized by mutual respect, shared understanding and assumptions, and efforts to work through conflicts constructively (Epstein, 2012; Pianta & Walsh, 1996).

Although the concept of partnership and how it is described imply something conscious and purposefully coordinated, that is not necessarily the case. Yes, the clearest example of family-school-community partnerships does fit this description. In past writings, I have referred to it as "direct partnership," characterized by knowing and goal-oriented attempts by parents, community members, and school personnel to talk and interact with each other (Crosnoe, 2012). Such direct partnership could take the form of parents frequently scheduling meetings with teachers in schools that regularly plan programs for parents and opportunities for parents, other community members, and school personnel to come together. All sides need to be active and engaged for this partnership to work, as the benefits of any one side will be diluted when not consistently matched by the others. Direct partnerships then facilitate the flow of academically and developmentally relevant information and support across the settings of children's daily lives. Such a flow would likely do more to introduce new and nonredundant resources to children from disadvantaged or disenfranchised families, thereby reducing academic and developmental disparities among young children related to their circumstances (Hoover-Dempsey & Sandler, 1997).

Not all partnerships are directly coordinated and maintained, which is why discussing what I have termed "indirect partnership" is also important. This term refers to the degree to which parents, educators, and community members are engaging children in enriching and supportive activities in their own context even if they are unaware of what is going on in other contexts. Indirect partnerships could take the form of parents organizing cognitively and socioemotionally stimulating activities for their children at home or in the community while teachers are scaffolding the development of critical thinking, academic, and socioemotional skills in their classrooms. The three sides need not be regularly coming together, but they form a triangle of academic and developmental supports that parallel and build off each other and allow children to enact and practice skills no matter where they are. Even though children from disadvantaged or disenfranchised populations are far less likely than other children to experience cognitive stimulation and other kinds of academic scaffolding across contexts, they stand to benefit the most when they do. Continuity in learning and developmental environments could mitigate many of the stressors and social and psychological risks of economic hardship and other structural and institutional disadvantages that disrupt learning, achievement, and development in this population. In these ways, the continuity could protect the children against the impact of factors that contribute to academic and developmental disparities across diverse groups (Crosnoe, 2012; Crosnoe et al., 2010; Magnuson et al., 2004; NICHD Early Child Care Research Network, 2002).

Whether direct or indirect, family-school-community partnerships protect children, while alienated, distant, or conflictual transactions among families, schools, and communities undermine, dilute, and sabotage their education. Parental involvement in education, therefore, can involve the same behaviors that play a very different role in children's learning, achievement, and development depending on how it is situated within these transactions. The degree to which parental involvement is situated in partnerships or in some other, less favorable transactions is not random but rather shaped by broad patterns of social stratification. The effects of that stratification are clear when looking at the Latina/o population.

Heightened Barriers to Partnerships for Latina/o Families

Building family-school-community partnerships and keeping these contextual systems in conversation are easier in some circumstances and harder in others, regardless of motivations to help young children or the value placed on their educational success. There are barriers to constructing those partnerships. Four general albeit far from universal factors at work in the Latina/o population and the schools that are supposed to serve them can be barriers between the two and make it harder to collaborate, sometimes without anyone even recognizing what is going on.

One such factor is socioeconomic status. The socioeconomic diversity within the Latina/o population extends to many middle-class and affluent Latina/o Americans whose numbers are growing. Yet, as a whole, Latina/o Americans are socioeconomically disadvantaged compared to the general population, with higher-than-average rates of poverty, less wealth accumulation, and relatively low levels of parental education. This contrast with the general population is even starker when considering the Latina/o families involved in public early childhood education programs; they tend to be among the most socioeconomically disadvantaged families in the country, to live in communities with high levels of concentrated poverty, and to be cut off from institutional services that could buffer them against such disadvantages (Hernandez et al., 2007; Pew Research Center, 2014; Turner et al., 2015).

Why does socioeconomic disadvantage matter to family-school-community partnerships? There are practical reasons for this link related to the lack of financial resources to purchase books and other goods and services for children and to lift constraints on parental involvement in education such as unpredictable transportation costs and inflexible work schedules. There is also a systematic disadvantage in a different kind of capital: human capital, the resources parents accrue through their own educational experiences including knowledge of the educational system and social status (Calzada et al., 2015; Cooper et al., 2010; Raver et al., 2007; Lareau, 2003).

Another factor is ethnicity. Latina/o is not a race, but it is a racialized status. That means it is widely viewed by Americans as a racial category. As such, it is subject to the forces of racial/ethnic stratification. Indeed,

Latina/o Americans are among the most segregated child groups within the US educational system in their schools and neighborhoods, and they suffer the consequences of that segregation when they attend underfunded and isolated schools. They and their families also are subject to differential treatment in schools, including explicit discrimination that limits their access to educational opportunities (Calzada et al., 2015; McWayne et al., 2013; Reardon & Owens, 2014).

Why does racial/ethnic treatment matter to family-school-community partnerships? One reason is that parents and other community members often face racial/ethnic stereotypes within schools of being uninvolved and valuing education less than other Americans; those biases can keep school personnel from reaching out to them as partners and keeps them from feeling comfortable or welcome in schools. It may also mean that school personnel do not see the ways parents are involved or give them credit for their involvement. That can occur even when the school personnel in question are Latina/o themselves, particularly when there is a socioeconomic divide between them and the families they serve. These kinds of problems are often invisible and implicit rather than overt, which makes it harder to identify and address them (Crosnoe, 2012; Adair & Tobin, 2008; Garcia Coll et al., 2002).

A third factor is language. Many Latina/o Americans, especially those with recent immigrant backgrounds and in immigrant-rich communities, do not speak English or are uncomfortable speaking English. More than three-quarters of the English language learners in US schools are Latina/o and speak Spanish as their first language. Texas has the second-highest proportion of English language learners in its student population among all states; the proportion is greater in urban school districts and among the youngest students (National Center for Education Statistics, 2019).

Why does language status matter to family-school-community partnerships? Since the business of the US educational system is primarily conducted in English and there is a shortage of Spanish-speaking educators in many schools, these language barriers in the home, school, and community can limit the degree to which parents know what is expected of them at school and school personnel know what parents want from them. They also disrupt the degree to which different actors can create and maintain meaningful dialogue and can discourage interaction overall. The conversation just becomes a lot harder unless there is some language broker, perhaps a bilingual teacher or counselor, who can help bring all sides together (Arzubiaga & Adair, 2009; Garcia Coll et al., 2002; Lopez et al., 2001; Suarez-Orozco & Suarez-Orozco, 2001; Tobin et al., 2013).

A final factor, culture, is intricately related to the other three. A Latina/o-focused critique of the concepts of parental involvement in education and family-school-community partnerships has evolved in recent decades that is anchored in a strength-based perspective rather than a deficit-based view. The strength-based critique holds that the basic assumptions by Latina/o families and by their children's school personnel about educational success do not always neatly line up, which keeps schools from effectively leveraging the resources that exist in their Latina/o students' families and communities. One concept that captures this perspective, *educación*, puts academic learning and moral development on equal footing as dimensions of education, which is not always in sync with the narrower academic conceptualization of education in US schools (Reese et al., 1995). This belief is part of long-standing cultural patterns of socialization found in many Latin American cultures. Different terms are used to describe the patterns, among them *respeto* (respect) and *bien educado* (well behaved), but they generally center on the idea that parents' paramount goal is to raise children who are good people (Valdés, 1996). Success can be seen in children who grow up to be obedient, deferential, well-behaved, and other-oriented and who give back to their communities, reflecting a socioecentric cultural orientation toward family (*familismo*) more than to individuals (Calzada et al., 2010; Harwood et al., 2010; Paredes et al., 2018; Rivas-Drake & Marchand, 2016).

Why does culture matter to family-school-community partnerships? Given cultural patterns, the engagement of parents of Latin American origin in the educational process often revolves around shaping the moral and ethical development of their children, to the extent that parents believe doing so is ultimately the best way to help their children succeed academically. In contrast, the script of parental involvement that predominates in US schools—with parents visibly engaged in school affairs and actively managing their children's academic activities—grows out of a different emphasis on a child's academic achievement as the barometer of the success of a parent's socialization. This cultural difference between many Latina/o parents and their children's schools can result in the former being written off as not caring about their children's educations and blamed for any academic setbacks their children face in school. Even when Latina/o parents enact what they believe to be the most effective form of parental involvement, they often are viewed by school personnel as uninvolved. It is, at heart, a misinterpretation because the two main actors are meeting across a cultural divide that may even happen with Latina/o teachers and Latina/o parents, depending on how much the teachers have been socialized into the parental involvement script (Paredes et al., 2018; Galindo & Sheldon, 2012; Reese et al., 1995; Valdés, 1996).

These four factors intersect to make the children of Latina/o parents and the parents themselves vulnerable in US schools, particularly in public schools and public early childhood education programs. Such parents and other members of their communities have many practical obstacles to being the kinds of visibly involved or even overinvolved parents and adults whom US schools tend to reward. Many of them have trouble putting in the time and money that this level and flavor of parental involvement entail or deciphering the unwritten rules underlying the demands and rewards. The parents also might have very different beliefs about the value of such involvement and the type of success it is supposed to support. Thus, there is a risk of disconnect or even conflict among families, communities, and schools (Adair & Tobin, 2008; McWayne et al., 2008; Lopez et al., 2001; Reese et al., 1995).

National-level disparities in family-school-community partnerships offer a frame in which any one study of these issues, including this study, plays out. I analyzed national data on kindergartners from the Early Childhood Longitudinal Study Kindergarten Cohort of 2010; the data were produced by the National Center for Education Statistics to follow a representative sample of kindergarteners through elementary school. I counted the number of school-based involvement activities reported by parents during the kindergarten year; they included attending school events, volunteering, and going to parent-teacher association meetings. Latina/o parents scored lowest on these counts by a significant degree. Their difference compared to non-Latina/o white parents was close to a full involvement activity lower across the year. To determine how meaningful this difference is, I followed conventional practice by converting the raw difference to standard deviation units on the full distribution of the measure in question. A standard deviation measures how much typical values diverge from the mean, the average, in a sample. An observed difference between a quarter and a half of standard deviation is often considered to be a moderate effect, while one exceeding half of a standard deviation tends to be viewed as a large effect. The Latina/o-white difference equaled about 40 percent of a standard deviation, and the difference between Latina/o and African American parents was even larger. Analyses of other relevant measures revealed the same pattern for parent-reported contact with schools and school-reported contact with parents, although these measures did not tap into the kinds of parental behaviors in line with concepts like *respeto* or *bien educado*.

The National Center for Education Statistics conducted a similar study following a nationally representative sample of infants born in 2001 into the start of elementary school. It is the Early Childhood Longitudinal Study

Birth Cohort. For the subsample of children who attended some early childhood education program before elementary school, I also analyzed data on families' interactions with schools. These patterns were less consistent in that there were some parent-reported and educator-reported activities on which Latina/o parents scored similar to or higher than white parents, such as attending parent-teacher meetings and program events. This discrepancy could reflect that the subsample of Latina/o parents who enrolled their children in voluntary early childhood education programs was more selective than the sample of Latina/o parents whose children attended mandatory elementary school. Relevant questions were what brought them to the program and whether that made them different from low-income Latina/o parents who did not find or access the program. Perhaps they were more comfortable in US educational settings or already had ties with the early childhood education program. The comparison of these two national pictures suggests that Latina/o parents may have had more trouble connecting with children's schools than other parents overall, but there is certainly a lot of variability within that pattern.

The creation and effectiveness of family-school-community partnerships requires a culturally informed perspective that recognizes the many seen and unseen threats of stratification that divide US society and lead to unequal interactions between powerful and vulnerable groups. This perspective, in turn, requires careful attention to identifying opportunities for building family-school-community partnerships and the practical, social, and cultural challenges to doing so; practical obstacles include time constraints and social and cultural differences in the ways US school personnel view education and the broader views of education held by parents (*educación*). Following a long tradition of qualitative research in this area (McWayne et al., 2013; Tobin et al., 2013), we pursued this goal by talking with and watching parents sending their children into public early childhood education and educators receiving their children. We paid special attention to the ways these two groups of adults talked to and past each other.

Learning from the Partners

The insights we gleaned from spending so much time in SWISD were primarily a result of the talking part of our investigative process. We relied heavily on interviews with teachers and parents rather than on the CLASS, which, by definition as a classroom observation system, does not explicitly involve parents or community members. We focused primarily on the teachers and parents of children in the pre-K classrooms of SWISD, including at the Cole Pre-K Campus, but we also examined data across all grades in case there might be grade-level trends after children leave pre-K. We drew on the portions of the teacher interviews that directly gauged issues of family-school-community relations; some came from prompts concerning how teachers saw the parents of their students and the parents' interactions with schools and participation in the educational process. Similarly, the relevant portions of the parent interviews concerned how parents interacted with and viewed school personnel and how they saw their roles in the educational careers of their children at home and in school.

In our data collection activities at SWISD, we began with some idea of the themes we wanted to explore when looking into family-school-community partnerships based on past research in this area, including my own. These a priori themes included expectations that teachers would interpret parents' engagement in schooling through a more psychological lens, such as a mother having or lacking some personal motivation, rather than a structural lens, such as a mother whose environmental circumstances constrained her or opened up opportunities. We expected that even seemingly engaged parent-teacher relations would have power imbalances that reduced their potential value and that parents and teachers would have stronger partnerships as they shared more social and demographic similarities such as language use and ethnicity. Just because we had reason to assume that these themes would be evident in SWISD does not mean that we were closed off to seeing other themes, what we call "emergent themes," or that we could not discern if our initial themes did not actually occur. We kept our eyes and ears open.

In revealing what Claude and I learned during this time in SWISD, I should note up front that teachers, other school personnel, and parents all tended to discuss the family component of family-school-community partnerships in a gender-neutral way. Yet, the way they discussed it indicated that for the most part, "parent" meant the mother, not the father or another partner. In practice, family-school-community partnerships were highly gendered.

Teachers, Parents, and Different Angles

Two people can see the same situation in different ways so that something seemingly objective becomes highly subjective. That is certainly the case with interactions between teachers and parents in early childhood education and the primary grades of elementary school.

What Teachers Think

A classroom at Cole populated by children from low-income Latina/o families in the SWISD pre-K program was unique in that it was co-taught by teachers of different ethnicities, Ms. Harris, who is white, and Ms. Torres, who is Latina, and it was designated as a Preschool Program for Children with Disabilities (PPCD). As a PPCD, it was a full-inclusion classroom for children with special needs such as needing extra assistance developing language and communication, social behavioral, or gross and fine motor skills. These two teachers were in agreement in almost every way except when it came to their perceptions of the role of parents in education. This exchange took place after Claude asked them whether their conceptions of parents' roles differed depending on the backgrounds of their students' parents:

> Ms. Harris: If you don't have parent involvement and it's a high social economic group, you're still going to have the same problem, but as far as where they come in at it, it is a lot easier.... And you know these other kids [compared to most children from economically disadvantaged families] that have had all these experiences, and Mom and Dad have been talking to them and what not, but they [more affluent parents] lost their jobs, therefore they qualify now [for special pre-K programs]. They come in and there's just loads of language [use at home]. I mean, so much language going on, so it does make a difference because for those kids I don't have to say, "This means 'cat.' This means 'stop.' This means ...." They know what those words mean. We are really able to build on different skills sets, but, you know, parts of it, no.
>
> Ms. Torres: Also, though, with that, I think there would be other issues if you had a higher socioeconomic classroom and even just with respect. ... This year alone, like we have one student in particular who is very high academically. We always have to keep reminding him to be more respectful and to really listen because, you know, sometimes the other students ... he's not on the same level with them academically. So he might get bored because we're going over a different word that he already knows the answer to or the definition of, and we have to kind of remind him, you know, other people need to learn too.... [They say,] "We'll get your stuff, what you need to learn," and we also need to get what they [other students] need to learn. So it just depends.

Ms. Harris emphasized large socioeconomic differences among their students, with socioeconomic advantages at home helping some children come into the classroom with more developed skills to build on than other students. The teachers tended to think of these advantages and disadvantages in terms of the learning environments parents constructed at home. Indeed, Ms. Harris said many children from socioeconomically disadvantaged families were more at the developmental level of an infant or toddler because their parents had not helped to scaffold their development at home. As a result, she thought their parents had pushed a greater burden on her, while their more advantaged peers had made her job easier. Ms. Torres did not exactly disagree with this assessment but also suggested that what she saw as the cognitive developmental edge of children from socioeconomically advantaged families also came with a socioemotional developmental deficit; in this difference she echoed ideas related to *respeto* and *bien educado*. By saying "It just depends," she was qualifying the idea that socioeconomic advantages led to home environments that positively supported the development of children across an array of domains for successful schooling.

Although these two teachers were in a unique teaching position in SWISD, the way they talked about parents reflected some of the tensions about family-school-community partnerships across social, economic, and demographic lines that are often more complicated than they seem on the surface. This exchange illustrated another striking feature of teacher discussions of family-school-community partnerships in SWISD that is likely to be quite common regardless of district; it is that teachers often discuss their students in ways that reflect on those children's parents. They imply or actually verbalize that some aspect of a student's classroom adjustment, behavior, or performance says something about the parents' general approach to parenting. For the most part, this tendency has a more explicitly or implicitly negative tone among white teachers and is more nuanced for Latina teachers. For example, Ms. Harris reported,

> Well, we give them the tools that they need [at] the very beginning of the year. We basically spell out exactly what we want them to achieve by the end of pre-K. Now, not all the parents utilize it, and we give them homework and we give them books to read, [books] they can take home. And you know, you can tell from the very beginning of the school year to the end which ones did their homework and which ones … you know, [which parents] follow[ed] through at home and which ones didn't by the progression of their child.

Again, Ms. Torres agreed with Ms. Harris but then went further in ways that deepened the discussion: "I think one thing that we do that might be different from other classrooms is every month we have a parent lunch, and we make a class movie of everything that the children have been learning throughout the month, and so we show it up on the screen and they get to come and interact with their kids and see what's been going on."

Ms. Torres was more likely to talk about parents themselves than to infer something from children about their parents. She emphasized the multilateral nature of partnerships by discussing her own role in eliciting the engagement of her students' parents, although she focused on her own conceptualization of what involvement entailed that may or may not have aligned with parents' conceptualizations. Ms. Harris immediately agreed with this sentiment, describing the various ways that she and Ms. Torres tried to invite and support the engagement of their students' parents, but she ended this description by bemoaning that some parents just did not participate in these activities. For her, the level of interaction between teacher and parent was about the parent more than it was about the teacher. In this classroom as well as across the classrooms we visited, Latina teachers tended to qualify and deepen discourses about family-school relations when discussing the Latina/o parents of their students. Non-Latina teachers, on the other hand, tended to speak in broader streams of thought that, regardless of their intentions, could be construed as critical or judgmental of parents.

What Parents Think

Teachers spoke to us a great deal about how they wanted more parental involvement in education and about what they needed from parents, but they rarely evoked the kind of language associated with the concept of and policy agenda surrounding partnerships of families, schools, and communities. Teachers rarely if ever referred to "partners" or "teams" when discussing parents and community members, while the use of such language was frequent and consistent among the students' mothers with whom we spoke in SWISD.[1]

In one focus group interview with Latina mothers, most of whom were immigrants, there was much nodding in agreement when a mother said she and her child's pre-K teachers made "a good team." Another mother reflected what she and her peers had learned from the Primeros Maestros (First Teachers) program for parents that stressed the value of complementary learning environments at home and school when she referred to her

---

1. Some of the mothers' comments in this section are used or discussed in condensed form in a 2015 article published in *International Journal of Family Psychology* (Crosnoe & Ansari, 2015). The quotations are translated from Spanish.

child as having "three teachers." She meant the child had two teachers at school plus her. This kind of talk was so pervasive that in one focus group discussion, some mothers even seemed to police one mother who was not using the "right" language to discuss home and school.

Latina mothers in SWISD espoused a view of teachers as equals, as part of the same team working together to help children. They also spoke in ways that rejected a common idea in the literature about Latina/o families that would paint them as more passive actors in relation to their children's schools. The concepts of Latina/o parental socialization such as *respeto*, *bien educado*, and *educación* generally are often interpreted as meaning that Latina/o immigrant parents view children's academic development as the school's responsibility and children's moral and social development as their parental responsibility in a more complementary rather than interactive connection between school and family roles. Yet, a broader interpretation is that Latina/o parents see the academic side of things as more shared with schools than the moral and social side. In line with this interpretation, the mothers we met made very strong claims that they were in charge of all aspects of their children's development and that ensuring that their children learned and developed academic skills was their duty.

Again, these views might have reflected the special sample of low-income Latina/o mothers. After all, they had found out about a voluntary enrollment early childhood education program in the district and got their children into it and then agreed to be a part of a study. What interested me more was how, when we dug deeper, the story seemed different or at least far more complicated. There appeared to be a disjunction between the label "team" or "partnership" and the actions to which they applied that label in their lives. When we got into the substance and details of their interactions with teachers and school personnel, we came to see that home learning activities were more supplementary to school learning activities than complementary or synergistic. Overwhelmingly, the mothers discussed their sides of family-school-community partnerships as helping children with their schoolwork and making sure that it was done in ways that seemed to be dictated by teachers. Although early childhood education is not like elementary school or later stages of schooling, the women's answers to questions about how they managed their children's educational progress or interacted with teachers were consistently centered on homework. One answered, "Send homework, so you can have something to do with them. I have noticed that if it's homework, it's easier for them to sit and study at home." Another responded, "[Have] conferences among teachers, parents, and principals, conferences where you talk more about the child, what he needs to learn, and what they're going to send home."

Teachers often answered in similar ways about what they want from parents. My focus on such answers is not to say that a concern about homework even in early childhood education is bad or that low-income Latina mothers need to become more like their more affluent white counterparts in being overly involved or even pushy in visible ways in schooling. A debate can and should be had about the pros and cons of each approach. I just want to point out how the concept of family-school-community partnerships takes a more one-sided form when moving from generalities to specifics on the part of parents and teachers. In these false partnerships, teachers direct everything and do it on their terms following prevailing school norms about what parents are supposed to be doing. It is not an exchange bur rather flows from school to home or community with little in return. Even when parents and teachers do talk, the conversation is about what teachers want parents to know and rarely about what parents want teachers to know; these talks tend to focus on academic topics rather than other aspects of children's lives. The parents' perspectives on children are rarely sought or shared, and there is little discussion about how parents could extend what is going on in school outside of school, or vice versa, through academic or developmental activities. In this way, the language of partnership or teamwork seems to obscure the power imbalance between home and school.

The low-income mothers with whom we spoke were largely young, Spanish-speaking women from immigrant backgrounds; they respected their children's teachers but did not feel connected to them. Although we were only able to tap into this emotion after some discussion, the respondents said they felt alone in helping their young children learn and achieve and develop. Their partners did not participate much in the day-to-day of child-rearing, and the respondents were often not well connected with other mothers shepherding their children into and through early childhood education and the primary grades. As a result, the mothers we interviewed found the whole process of sending their children into school a bit isolating, and that isolation was exacerbated by an often unspoken but apparent sense that teachers and other school personnel were intimidating.

I want to be clear that the disjunction between the value placed on family-school-community partnerships and the ways those partnerships manifested was not simply a function of language differences between parents and teachers. We saw it even with Spanish-speaking mothers matched with Spanish-speaking, usually Latina teachers and with English-speaking mothers matched with English-speaking teachers. It appeared to be more reflective of socioeconomic differences, often layered with ethnic differences as well, and the inequality that often colors interactions between advantaged people with power on the inside and disadvantaged people who lack power on the outside.

Teachers' Socioeconomic and Racialized Views of Parents

The insights into teachers' and parents' views of family-school-community partnerships revealed one fundamental difference in these two sets of important adults in children's lives. Teachers were much more likely to openly interpret the motivations, values, and behaviors of parents, often in negative ways, while parents could discuss at length their experiences with teachers without trying to explain them. For this reason, I want to focus on what Claude and I learned from teachers about how they tried to make sense of their students' parents. Overwhelmingly, their interpretations and perceptions were colored by issues of socioeconomic status and race/ethnicity. These issues often manifested in the idea among teachers that parents who did not follow the views of parental involvement predominant in schools did not care about education rather than the possibility that they might have different and often complementary views about education.

Teachers' Perceptions of Socioeconomic Barriers and Deficits

When talking about their students' low-income Latina/o parents, teachers invariably discussed how the parents' socioeconomically disadvantaged circumstances, as well as those of other community members, seemed to make it harder for them to partner with schools. This could be construed as their recognition of the barriers that only some parents face, and initially it seemed to be a departure from their tendency to explain parental behavior in terms of individual motivations and values. As these discussions progressed, however, it became clearer that the teachers often viewed low socioeconomic status not as a structural barrier to partnering with schools but rather as a window into the poor as people.

Ms. Kellerman taught a pre-K class in a gentrifying but still socioeconomically and racially/ethnically diverse community. The class was in a dual language instruction school called Teller that attracted a broad array of families. Her class was more mixed than others we visited, and socioeconomic issues were especially salient in this context. Ms. Kellerman seemed to recognize that her classroom was a microcosm of societal inequality at large, but she also occasionally slipped into a way of talking about family socioeconomic status that was more interpersonal and individual than her recognition of inequality implied. The following exchange she had with Claude begins with a consideration of disruptive students: "As a teacher you don't want to let anybody down, but when there's a student who really has no self-control and is interrupting . . . the class all the time, you know, you have to look for strategies to deal with them but also keep all these other kids engaged and working on something."

When Claude suggested a connection between socioeconomically disadvantaged backgrounds and such behavior, Ms. Kellerman initially agreed but then continued in a way that seemed to undermine his drawing this line. She also seemed to resist his attempts to suggest that this scenario could happen with both socioeconomically disadvantaged and advantaged children:

> No, I mean I have one that's high SES [socioeconomic status] who has low self-control, but you know having those variables, and I think that there are some students who have low SES who are . . . that doesn't affect how their parents and their parents' culture, teaching them control and teaching them good manners and all of that. But there are some that, you know . . . there's also like, well, I guess like you were saying, there's a cultural [component], like I've been exposed to the zoo and I've been exposed to, you know, all kinds of different places, and I go out and I hike every weekend, and I, as opposed to a lot of . . . unfortunately, a lot of the low-SES students . . . [who] go home and watch TV all evening or go home and play video games all weekend.

As this conversation continued, Ms. Kellerman recalled how she had been raised in a middle-class family. She suggested that her own parents had given her more stimulating and rewarding experiences than her students, not just because they had the money to do so but simply because they wanted to do so. She seemed to imply that there was a level of choice involved, and she did not dwell on practical barriers to those kinds of parenting behaviors or that video game play might be related to socioeconomic status in more complicated ways. She also did not seem critical of the idea that academics-focused parenting behavior was the primary or only way to shape a child for academic success.

Almost all teachers we met with during our time at SWISD recognized that socioeconomic disadvantages on the level of family or community could mean that children would have less opportunity to learn and achieve in and out of school. Still, many, including Ms. Kellerman, tended to see this connection in terms of what parents thought or wanted rather than what they could or could not do. For these teachers, it was about something internal to parents rather than related to outside forces such as inequality.

Other teachers who were themselves Latina also tended to dwell on socioeconomic explanations when discussing low-income Latina/o parents' relations with school. Yet, when they did, they had a more empathetic way of discussing parents. Two dual-language program teachers, Ms. Fernandez, in the same school as Ms. Kellerman, and Ms. Figueroa, in a different school, O'Connor Elementary, expressed their thoughts.

> Ms. Fernandez: A lot of times our parents, even if they wanted to, they couldn't. They were in a survivor mode. They were too busy trying to survive. They didn't or they were working the evenings or they were, you know, it was hard for them. But now this recent rule with the dual language program [parents could pay for it if they were not eligible for free preschool], we've had some children that come from two-parent homes, [and] sometimes the mom is a stay-home mom, and so they have more support.... It's not an ethnic thing. I think it's more an economic thing. Because some of the other children come from single-parent homes, and it's hard.
>
> Ms. Figueroa: Unfortunately, I think a lot of our parents have two or three jobs sometimes, and they don't have a lot [of] time at home with, they don't spend a lot of time at home with their students. And I'm speaking for most of my students, not all of them. I do have some [parents] who are very active and encourage the students to just pretty much push a little beyond what they are actually doing. And I think that's great, but a lot of them do not have the time to meet with our students because of work or simply because they don't know how to.

Ms. Fernandez also said she needed to "stay on top" of the situation to help struggling parents participate in the schooling process in ways that their more socioeconomically advantaged counterparts could on a more consistent basis. For her part, Ms. Figueroa identified what she saw as lower levels of school participation among low-income Latina/o parents, but she did not blame them for it or explain it as a deficiency. Like Ms. Fernandez, she also recognized that many of the parents were in a hard spot.

The Racialization of Parental Involvement

Across the board, teachers and other school personnel were much more likely to discuss their perceptions of the involvement of their students' parents in terms of socioeconomic status than race/ethnicity. Race/ethnicity, however, was often just under the surface of these discussions, not always articulated but still easy to infer or discern. White teachers were much more likely to avoid directly addressing issues of race/ethnicity, perhaps out of a concern that they would be viewed by us as racist.[2] Instead, they seemed to equate Latina/o status with other kinds of hardships and risks, as if the conditions naturally went together and could not be separated, and to talk about diversity as mixing haves with have nots. The following thoughts were shared by three white teachers—one at Cole, the others on site in their elementary schools—serving largely but not completely Latina/o classrooms:

> Parent involvement is just as important to that child as my involvement. Then, obviously they need to be learning while they're at home, too, but they need to see the congruency between me and their parents, how much water ... what I say holds, ... how much water it holds with me, but also with the parent. Like we need to be on the same level, that's what's going ... to give the most success to a child. Straight up, that's all it is. But it's hard because we never see them. It's really hard. You know, and their phone numbers change every other week, and you know what I mean, and it's just a very ... it's just that demographic, it's tough to communicate, and they have a lot of stress in their lives and, yeah.
>
> Some of them mention it [incarceration] like it is so normal, you know. "Oh yeah my dad is in jail too. How long has your dad been in jail? When is he getting out?" You know, so it's definitely more challenging because I feel like you do get some more, like, behavior problems, and I definitely feel like, as opposed to a school that, you know, has more, like, involved families and higher income. They come in more on grade level. I think at a school like ours we get a lot more of that, that's really challenging.
>
> I don't know, to me I think it would be boring if they were like all rich white kids, they were all like smart [*laughs*]. You know? So it's funny because I have like one white girl in my class, she does stand out [*laughs*]. And she's

---

2. The reluctance of white teachers to explicitly engage with issues of race/ethnicity out of a concern for how they will be viewed is related to the concept of "color muteness" (Pollock, 2004).

extremely intelligent and she's really funny, the things she says, the way she talks. And then, so, I have, like, her, and then I have a bunch of gifted and talented kids, probably about five that are really, really intelligent and above grade level. And then I have a bunch of, you know, on level, and then I have two that are, like, extremely below and then a couple below. So you know, it's definitely a big range, and that's probably one of my biggest challenges, meeting all of their needs.

In the eyes of these white teachers, Latina/o parents were generally uninvolved, and it was not so much because they were Latina/o as because of all the other things that being Latina/o signified to them. They categorized children and their parents simplistically, making it harder for them to think about parents contributing to family-school-community partnerships.

Latina/o teachers often touched on race/ethnicity in much more nuanced ways that could be favorable or unfavorable and that tended to be more about cultural differences, without judgment, than about potential cultural deficits. Latina/o teachers, two at Cole and the other on site in an elementary school, brought up issues of Latina/o culture, echoing *respeto, bien educado*, and so on, when discussing their relations with Latina/o parents and how visibly involved the parents were in the school process:

I would have to really get to know those cultures and, like, if you're talking about parent involvement I mean I'm not, I don't know how other cultures see that, like, is from their culture is it okay for them to be in the classroom or what the views are in those cultures.

In the Hispanic culture, so far that I've seen, parents see education as something very important and they assist the teachers. I mean not as much as I wish to, because again they're new in parenting, but they have the general concept that education is something that is going to be of benefit to the students, and they try to have their kids to follow through and be good students.

To me it seems like it is a cultural thing. It's that whole "respeto de la maestro," that respecting the teacher, respecting the school. It's like, you know, I'm like a mini little goddess for them, and it's very nice [*laughs*]. But at the same time, it's also very helpful to me because they understand where I'm coming from, they understand that if they do their part their child is only going to move forward.... I do make a lot of effort to build relationships with parents, and I do tend to put a little bit of pressure on them, but at the same time it's not pressure that, you know, they probably don't put on themselves already.

These and other Latina/o teachers recognize likely differences between Latina/o culture and the white middle-class culture that tends to dominate the US educational system, but they do not equate one as better than the other. That view is very much in the spirit of the work of Guadalupe Valdés (1996) that helped open up research on Latina/o parenting to more strength-based perspectives. The teachers try to understand these differences and work with or around them while giving credit where it is due.

In sum, white teachers who talked with us tended to avoid explicitly discussing race/ethnicity and culture in relation to their students or their students' parents; they did often use socioeconomic status or related circumstances as a means of drawing disparaging generalizations about them. Latina teachers were less reluctant to discuss race/ethnicity and culture, but their thoughts on them were also more complicated and less consistently negative. They also expressed an enthusiasm or sense of obligation to bridge cultural divides as they saw them.

This racial/ethnic theme added depth to our research in that teachers' perceptions about socioeconomic barriers often highlighted the personal over the structural and were likely tinged with an inability to separate socioeconomic status from race/ethnicity. Furthermore, the greater sympathy and empathy of Latina teachers toward Latina/o parents, relative to the teachers' white counterparts, was not exclusively confined to how they saw race/ethnicity but extended to other disadvantaged statuses in the educational system.

Families, Schools, and Communities Partnered at a Remove

For some time, family-school-community partnerships have been at the top of the list of policies and practices invoked when discussing how to address socioeconomic and demographic inequalities in schooling; the thought is that bringing all the adults in students' lives together as a team is the key to helping all children do better. The advantages of such partnerships, the thinking also goes, will be more redundant for students who already have other kinds of advantages than it will be for students without access to as many resources, thereby leveling the playing field. This strong emphasis on family-school-community partnerships as a potential remedy for educational inequality has extended to the Latina/o population, given the convergence of sociodemographic disadvantages and cultural barriers in this population that can block students from educational opportunities and keep their parents at a remove from schools. It has also extended from K-12 education into early childhood education, from the strong sense that parents play a particularly integral role in getting children ready for and comfortable in schools.

Our time in SWISD talking with Latina mothers and their children's teachers revealed that this emphasis on family-school-community partnerships is often too simplistic and that greater awareness is needed of the complicated challenges that could get in the way of making this strategy work in US schools. Parents like the partnership language and buy into it, but they are often at a loss as to how to actually forge partnerships or what they might entail. They fall or are pushed into much more unidirectional, power-imbalanced relations with teachers in which they are objects more than subjects and their strengths are not recognized. Teachers are much more likely to fall back on the idea of parental involvement in education that used to be the buzzy idea in educational research and policy before the emergence of family-school-community partnerships. At the same time, teachers tend to view parental involvement in education as an internally driven rather than externally influenced behavior that does not really depend on them or the school. That tendency is especially challenging when it undercuts awareness of real and practical barriers to Latina/o parents' engagement in the same kinds of involvement behaviors as white middle-class parents and when teachers also make racial/ethnic assumptions about parents. Racial/ethnic matching between teachers and parents can ease some of these challenges but cannot eliminate them, perhaps because of the intersectionality of race/ethnicity, socioeconomic status, and other markers of inequality and perhaps simply because parents and teachers are more likely to view through a critical lens what others are doing than what they themselves are doing.

Identifying challenges like these also helps to identify opportunities. There are ways forward to build family-school-community partnerships around young Latina/o children from low-income backgrounds within the context of early childhood education. There is a real value in community-based discussions about the best ways to help address the practical barriers to forming such partnerships. For example, if scheduling around constricted and unpredictable work schedules is an issue, schools' participation in these discussions could lead to the implementation of more flexible policies about when and where outreach and involvement activities take place. Or if linguistic barriers are keeping parents and teachers from being on the same page, funds might be diverted to hiring support for translators or providing bilingual training for school personnel. Many people seem to recognize that these practical barriers exist, but little action is taken on them even though they could be addressed concretely.

Another opportunity lies in the need for translation, but in the figurative sense more than the literal sense of going back and forth between Spanish and English. Those on each side think they know the other, but clearly they often see past each other and the assumptions about what each does. What they need is to engage in moderated group discussions led by an actor who knows both sides and can help them ask the right questions of each other and discern what the other needs to know. That means helping demystify the often unwritten rules of US education about parents' role in schooling for parents and helping school personnel grasp what families want and expect from them. At the Cole Pre-K Campus, I watched a very committed Spanish-speaking Latina parent-support specialist do just that with both sides. The limitation was that she did it first with the parents and then separately with the teachers, when the real value would be in bringing everyone together.

I believe parents and community members should be actively involved in schooling and schools should recognize that part of their job is to elicit and support that involvement. I do not mean that I think that the kinds of active, visible, and demanding forms of parental involvement in education so closely associated with the white middle class are some sort of standard by which parental involvement in education is judged. I personally find those norms to be hard to take and to live up to in my personal life as a parent despite the advantaged resources and status I bring with me into schools as a middle-class, non-Latino, white man. I also am unconvinced that there is inherent value in those forms of parental involvement in education other than that they line up well with what school personnel expect and equate with good parenting. Thus, in moving forward with efforts to build family-school-community partnerships that facilitate the educational involvement of low-income Latina/o parents as a means of helping their children succeed, we also need to problematize our own images of parental involvement in education and the many different ways that it can take shape.

CHAPTER 4

Connecting Academic and Socioemotional Goals

The "between-context" connections derived from contextual systems theory are those in which different contexts of social life come together (or not) to support (or not) the educational experiences of young children from low-income Latina/o families at the starting line. I turn now to the "within-context" connections part of the blueprint. These connected processes refer to the ways that any one context of social life—in this case, the classroom—is itself made up of interrelated parts that may help or hurt young children from this growing but highly disadvantaged population succeed in the US educational system.

Ideally, the different components of an early childhood education classroom are "in conversation" with each other, to use the term from contextual systems theory, so that the whole is greater than the sum of the parts. Less ideally, and moving away from the theory, there may be early childhood education classrooms in which only some components are active and developed. In other classrooms all components may be at work but in conflict with each other. There are, of course, many ways to think about the components of early childhood education classrooms and just as many ways to think about how these components may be in conversation or conflict with each other. To set up my particular exploration of connected processes within classrooms, I start with connected instructional philosophies. To do so, I am going back to a key debate in early childhood education about developmentally appropriate practices versus the standards movement and the argument that this is a false dichotomy with much middle ground between the two poles.

The falsity of this debate is that the two poles have been so separated

Aida Ramos collaborated with me on this chapter.

out that one (developmentally appropriate practices) is thought to singularly emphasize socioemotional development while the other (standards and accountability) is thought to singularly emphasize academic achievement. The middle ground is that academic activities are important to learning and social development, that such activities can be constructed to support the needs of children and various points of development, and that successful classrooms provide such developmentally informed academic activities in the context of ample support for social and emotional development (Ryan & Grieshaber, 2005). This middle ground can be further leveraged for support of children by also recognizing and addressing a point of criticism that has been levied at both poles, which is that they are often not practiced in culturally responsive ways. Indeed, tailoring classroom activities, whether more academically or developmentally focused, to meet children where they are and align with their cultural contexts is a method to capitalize on the middle ground (Brown & Lan, 2015; Fuller et al., 2017; Le et al., 2019; National Association for the Education of Young Children, 2019).

At the heart of this discussion is the need to educate the "whole child" and the belief that young children's ultimate academic prospects are best served by fostering positive development across a wide array of domains. Those domains include cognitive and socioemotional development, mastering new skills, learning about oneself and the world, and regulating one's own behavior, effort, and interactions. Attending to the whole child need not be soft or insufficiently academic, and it need not come at the expense of the hard skills they will need to master their future schoolwork. Educating the whole child requires the construction of classroom environments that are both cognitively stimulating and socioemotionally nurturing, not to mention culturally responsive, to help young children learn, develop in positive ways, and meet the variety of challenges and demands they will face in school. These goals go together (Adair, 2014; Genishi & Dyson, 2009; Graue, 2008; National Association for the Education of Young Children, 2019).

A high-quality early childhood education classroom, therefore, covers all of the bases rather than being high-quality only in this way or that, and it does so with attention to both developmental needs and cultural context. As the public early childhood education movement across the country and in Texas strives not just to offer early educational opportunities to all children but to ensure that these opportunities encompass high-quality learning experiences, this philosophical concept of what quality means becomes important to consider and assess. That is what another of my graduate students, Aida Ramos, and I tried to do during our time in the SWISD pre-K program. To that end, we used the watching part of our approach to identify classrooms that were socioemotionally supportive and cognitively stimulating, those that leaned one way or the other, and those that were low on both. We then used the listening part to elucidate teachers' strategies, experiences, and perceptions and the larger institutional settings that supported or undermined the construction and maintenance of well-rounded pre-K classrooms serving the unique needs and circumstances of Latina/o children from low-income families.

Different Components of Quality Classrooms

The incredible push toward public investment in early childhood education has more recently focused on young children from low-income Latina/o families. In many ways, this dramatic shift in educational policy and funding has primarily been directed toward the expansion of opportunities for early enrichment. It has largely involved attempts to increase the number of children, including young children from low-income Latina/o families, enrolled in formal early childhood education programs and to even out long-standing socioeconomic, racial/ethnic, and immigration-related disparities in enrollment. The guiding idea has been that some inequalities in K-12 schooling reflect that young children from historically disadvantaged and disenfranchised segments of the US population have been disproportionately less likely to attend any kind of preschool program before kindergarten. As a result, they tend to start off behind their peers and then, reflecting the cumulative nature of the system, have trouble catching up and fall further behind (Duncan & Magnuson, 2013; Fuller, 2007; Lee & Burkham, 2002).

The public investment in early childhood education has promoted educational opportunity in this sense. Evidence shows a decreasing magnitude of social, economic, and demographic disparities in early childhood education enrollment in general and an increasing rate of enrollment of young children from low-income Latina/o families in particular. Certainly, the programs are not yet at a point of equal opportunity, but they have made progress (Karoly & Gonzalez, 2011; Mendez et al., 2018).

The early childhood education movement has expanded the issue of opportunity beyond enrollment per se to considerations of exposure to high-quality learning environments. More children from diverse walks of life are now entering early childhood education programs, but whether they are entering programs that will really help them get a jump start on K-12 schooling is still something of an unknown. After all, rising and more evenly distributed enrollment in early childhood education will only have the intended downstream effects on disparities in long-term academic achievement and educational attainment if children from diverse groups are experiencing the same levels and kinds of enrichment. To that end, greater attention is being given to what is going on inside early childhood education programs serving children from historically disadvantaged populations, including young children from low-income Latina/o families. They are enrolled, but is that enrollment giving them what they need? What do they need? Answering such questions requires consideration of different philosophies of children's early development and learning and the ways these philosophies may manifest in early childhood education classrooms (Crosnoe et al., 2015; Fuller, 2007; Mendez et al., 2018).

Developmentally Informed and Academically Focused Education

Although early childhood education has many goals and serves children in various ways, the explicit mission of most public early childhood education initiatives, including those in Texas, is to boost the school readiness of children. Typically, that mission is focused on children from groups that statistically have tended to demonstrate lower levels of academic readiness upon entering school.

Contrary to popular opinion, school readiness does not have a set and agreed-upon definition, as children can be ready for K-12 schooling in some ways but not in others. Different conceptions of school readiness prioritize different early childhood education approaches. The simplest definition of "school readiness" is the strictest, which is that children need to have some baseline level of cognitive and academic skills when they enter kindergarten to be able to engage with the kindergarten curriculum. This academic definition of school readiness prioritizes the goal of children being adequately prepared to begin that challenge at the starting line; early childhood education should be oriented toward that end. Thus, if reading instruction is to be a major goal of kindergarten activities in a district, children there need to have good phonics awareness prior to entering kindergarten in order to be school ready (Bassok et al., 2016; Fuller et al., 2017; Meisels, 2007; Takanishi, 2004). This conception of school readiness suggests a specific way that early childhood education programs in the district should be pedagogically organized and their effectiveness evaluated. In this sense, high-quality classrooms are those that consistently achieve this goal for their students.

Because schooling is a monumental task for children that will dominate their current and future lives, it requires a lot from students, especially very young students, that goes beyond academic proficiencies and cognitive assets (Weisberg et al., 2013). Yes, phonics awareness is an important foundation for learning, but it is not the sole foundation. Even a student who enters kindergarten with good phonics awareness might struggle in classroom reading activities if she or he does not have the social and emotional skills that promote learning in that context, such as an eagerness to learn, perseverance in the face of challenges, an ability to interpersonally connect with teachers and peers, and the self-regulation necessary to stay engaged and on task (Bierman et al., 2008; Blair & Raver, 2015; Howes et al., 2008; Raver, 2002). An early childhood education classroom could help children be school ready in theory, as in building one piece of the foundation, but not in reality, as in building multiple pieces of the foundation. With this expanded concept of school readiness encompassing the development of academic, cognitive, social, and emotional skills needed to engage in formal schooling, early childhood education classroom quality can have a more holistic feel than simply the delivery of academic instruction or the rigor of academic curricula.

Some do not buy this expanded conception of school readiness and believe that districts should stick to assessing school readiness in terms of concretely definable academic goals and directly measurable cognitive and academic skills. There are plenty of people in this camp, including many who are writing and funding educational policy. Like many others have, I would argue that expanding how we think about the quality of early childhood education programs is still necessary for ensuring that more children get school ready in this sense. To explain why, I return to that strict and, I admit, overly simplistic example of defining school readiness in terms of strong phonics awareness. Quality early childhood education programs would then be those that help their students meet this definition of school readiness. Yet, such programs would need to do more than just competently structure and support phonics awareness instruction and learning activities to help children become school ready in this way. They would also need to help the children be broadly prepared to engage in these activities, with sufficient interest, preparation, confidence, and shared sense of purpose. A quality early childhood program, therefore, would need to support students' acquisition of cognitive and academic skills while nurturing their development of the social and emotional skills that both support that acquisition and make it count (Bierman et al., 2008; Miller & Almon, 2009; Raver, 2002).

My point is that whether school readiness is defined in a strict academic sense or more broadly in terms of the full experience of schooling, the goals of helping children be school ready are served by threading together the social and emotional with cognitive and academic domains of early childhood development within educational settings. Following this philosophy leads to the idea that the unique developmental demands and opportunities of early childhood require a more holistic approach to the goals of early childhood education programs, expanded views of school readiness, and reoriented values about how an early childhood education classroom should look. High-quality classrooms would actively and purposively facilitate children's social and emotional development without sacrificing goals of academic school readiness or diluting learning activities designed to achieve these goals (Weisberg et al., 2013). Again, it does not advocate or accept an either/or proposition but instead focuses on the "and."

At the starting line, this philosophy prioritizes early childhood education classrooms that are socioemotionally supportive *and* academically scaffolding regardless of how school readiness is defined. With this prioritization, children from historically disadvantaged and disenfranchised segments of the population need more opportunities to enroll in early childhood education programs, particularly opportunities to enroll in programs that capture the essence of that "and." That is how educational inequality can be reduced through early childhood intervention.

The Special Case of Young Latina/o Children

A major reason Texas is a bellwether of the early childhood education movement is the extra attention the state program devotes to Latina/o students. While this movement focuses on children from communities that are economically and socially marginalized and suffer educationally as a result, young Latina/o children require extra attention. They are at heightened risk of economic, linguistic, immigration-related, and ethnic-based challenges, disadvantages, segregation, and differential treatment that cut across many systems of social stratification while also having an enormous and growing presence in the population. Thus, while young Latina/o children have some stake in almost any thread of discussion about early childhood education, they also invariably have a unique experience. That is certainly the case in discussions of the value of holistic concepts of school readiness and early childhood education quality, which require cultural responsiveness.

The shift toward stricter academic foci within the surge of public investment in early childhood education across many states has been acutely felt by children from low-income Latina/o families. Research conducted by the sociologist Bruce Fuller in California has documented the tensions between policy makers and Latina/o communities as early childhood education is increasingly conceived and sold as the replication of the K-12 academic system in the early school years (Fuller, 2007). Accompanying much greater funding for early childhood education, a growing emphasis has been placed on moving young Latina/o children into more formalized educational settings from community-based child care programs, which often provided more socioemotionally nurturing environments for children. The formal programs also were more closely organized around academic curricula, serving students more narrowly as pupils rather than more generally as children. Fuller has argued (2007) that this trend increased the rigor of academic instruction for many young children from low-income Latina/o families. Yet, disconnecting early childhood education and early child care from diverse immigrant communities and the linguistic and cultural practices that developed within them also created a problematic push and pull dynamic. It meant that many such children lost out on equally valuable developmental opportunities while gaining these academic opportunities and that other children received neither socioemotional nor academic support.

The value of culturally grounded classroom experiences linking academic learning and socioemotional development is echoed in the pioneering work of the early childhood education scholars Celia Genishi and Anne Dyson on young English language learners, who make up a large share of Latina/o children. Their research makes the case that the increasing emphasis on testing and accountability raises the risks that English language learners will be labeled as having deficits early in their educational careers regardless of their actual or potential skills. These labels then restrict their current and future opportunities to learn and achieve, a circumstance that calls for recognition of cultural connections and disconnections between children and the people teaching them (Genishi & Dyson, 2009). Social learning requires that teachers interact with children in ways that reflect an awareness of the children's cultural and language backgrounds, how they and their families communicate, and the value of maintaining their home language while learning a new one. Thus, just supporting young students in general is not enough; each child needs support in unique ways based on who that child is and where that child comes from.

Finding the middle ground between the perhaps seemingly but not truly distinct academic and developmental poles of early childhood education when crossing ethnic and socioeconomic lines is actually more complicated when it comes to Latina/o parents and educators. The anthropological research of Joseph Tobin, Jennifer Adair, and Angela Arzubiaga (2013) reveals this complexity. It recognizes that the socioemotional components of such practices and the valuing of informal learning activities such as through play often seem impractical and even counterproductive to people with experience in many Latin American educational systems. In these systems, such practices are less common or at least less explicitly sold as part of the curriculum. As a result of the novelty, Latina/o immigrant parents may be confused by early childhood education programs that to them do not look academic enough. The work also strikingly illustrates how many Latina/o immigrant teachers feel the same way when they start their jobs, go through an on-the-job process of forced forgetting of what they know, but still struggle with tensions between their old and new knowledge (Tobin et al., 2013). The value of holistic approaches to early childhood education needs to prompt stronger attempts at outreach and buy-in in many Latina/o communities.

Thus, early childhood education classrooms that are socioemotionally supportive and academically scaffolding prepare children for the multifaceted ways they will be engaged and challenged in the K-12 system. This preparatory space is less likely to come by yet more important for young children from low-income Latina/o families. Identifying which children are exposed to this resource, the different ways it can manifest in daily classroom processes, and what is standing in the way of facilitating it from being actualized in early childhood education programs is a way of expanding educational opportunities for this important and growing population.

Classrooms in Conversation

If classrooms organized around activities and interactions with a strong connection between social and emotional development and academic and cognitive development may boost the short-term and long-term prospects of young children from low-income Latina/o families, then surveying the landscape of early childhood education classrooms for such cross-philosophy connections is important. To do so, we need to think about what such cross-philosophy connections within classrooms might look like in the real world, map whom they serve, and wade into the thorny issues about where they are likely to emerge and what might be keeping them from emerging.

Conceptualizing Classrooms for the Whole Child

To say that classrooms should be socioemotionally supportive and academically scaffolding is one thing, but specifying how classrooms live up to these labels is another. How would such a classroom actually appear to a visitor?

By socioemotionally supportive, I mean that early childhood education classrooms should be structured to help young children forge *positive* interpersonal connections with adults and each other. The goal of these interpersonal connections is for the children to come to better understand themselves and the world around them. All of that should happen while the setting also fosters a sense of safety and security for young children and enables them to face challenges. Such classrooms nurture children and help them realize their own potential. To identify socioemotionally supportive classrooms, therefore, one would see an abundance of activities and interactions characterized by warmth, respect, and sensitivity with children as the central focus, a flexible openness to new ways of doing things mixed with firm behavioral and academic expectations, and a balance between being adult-directed and child-driven (Bierman et al., 2008; Howes et al., 2008; NICHD Early Child Care Research Network, 2005).

By "academically scaffolding," I mean early childhood education classrooms structured to help young children gradually acquire cognitive and academic skills that promote their future educational attainment. That skill development can come through the provision of rich early learning opportunities and concrete classroom supports for positive brain development. Through play, formal lessons, and less formal interactions, these classrooms enable children to develop representational thought, memory, attention, and self-regulation while also gaining new bases of knowledge such as words, numbers, and geography and expanding and deepening their language use. They stimulate young children to help them realize their potential. To identify academically scaffolding classrooms in programs and schools, therefore, one would probably want to see an abundance of activities and interactions involving complex language, consistent introduction of new ideas, rich discussion of information, efforts to encourage more abstract and analytical thinking, and attempts to connect what is happening in the classroom with the outside world. As with socioemotional support, academic scaffolding features of classrooms should encourage exchanges between children and adults and among children (Anderson & Phillips, 2017; Gathercole & Baddeley, 2014; NICHD Early Child Care Research Network, 2005; Pianta et al., 2018).

With these concepts of socioemotional support and academic scaffolding in an early childhood education setting, a well-rounded, high-quality classroom in an early childhood education program would be one in which children engage with a formal and informal curriculum and interact with and connect to others in ways that allow them to learn, mature, feel confident, and have fun.

Identifying Classrooms for the Whole Child

The CLASS is well-suited to figuring out how early childhood education classrooms mix and match elements of socioemotional support and academic scaffolding for young children. We conducted the CLASS in so many classrooms in SWISD as the watching part of data collection in the district to gain insights into how that mixing and matching plays out in an early childhood education program primarily serving children from low-income Latina/o families. Although we conducted CLASS in classrooms across grade levels, Aida and I decided to focus our exploration of whole-child classrooms on the pre-K year in SWISD, given that the balance of socioemotional and academic elements of education is expected to evolve in developmentally appropriate ways as children age and move through the system. Some of these 36 pre-K classrooms were housed at the Cole Pre-K Campus, while others were housed in elementary schools; observing both settings offered some perspective on how the institutional context of early childhood education may shape the organization and experience of each.

Basically, we set out to use the CLASS to identify classrooms with elements of both socioemotional support and academic scaffolding, those that did not consistently demonstrate elements of either, and those featuring elements of one more clearly than the other. Table I.1 presents the three main dimensions and subdimensions of CLASS as well as the primary indicators of each subdimension. Although we took all parts of the CLASS into account, we were particularly interested in the emotional and instructional support dimensions. The emotional support dimension encompasses positive elements of an overall classroom interpersonal climate, the absence of negative elements of that climate, and teachers' sensitivity toward children and regard for children's perspectives. The instructional support dimension encompasses activities and interactions that facilitate children's concept development and are characterized by teachers' use of high-quality feedback and language modeling. To delve deeper into the details of the CLASS, a classroom that is both socioemotionally supportive and academically scaffolding would be one that features respectful relations between children and teachers; teachers would be aware of what is going on with children even when not interacting with them. Teachers would foster children's sense of autonomy, encourage them to analyze and reason, and provide feedback on what they are doing in mutual and open-ended conversation (Pianta, LaParo, & Hamre, 2007).

We engaged in the CLASS observational process to rate each of the SWISD classrooms on all subdimensions and aggregated these ratings to reach a score for each of the three dimensions. For this exercise we went a step further by using the ratings to sort the 36 pre-K classrooms into groups with different configurations across the three domains.[1] This process resulted in three basic configurations, each representing a group of classrooms that looked similar in how the central dimensions of the CLASS came together within them. For example, two classrooms might have been similar in emotional support but land in different clusters in the typology because emotional support was coupled with low instructional support in one and high instructional support in the other. What mattered was the configuration of classroom processes, not any one process on its own.

Before presenting these configurations, we wanted to provide some help with interpreting them. To that end, we can use the national averages on the CLASS in early childhood education classrooms as a benchmark (Pianta, LaParo, & Hamre, 2007). At the national level, scores on the emotional support domain reflect a bell-shaped curve that centered on the medium to high threshold (score 4–6). For classroom organization, the bell shape is anchored on the higher side of the middle range (3–5), and for instructional support, the bell shape is centered within the low range (1–2). In other words, early childhood education classrooms in the United States, including many public pre-K classrooms, tend to be much higher on emotional support than instructional support, and they tend to be quite low on the latter overall.

Three Types of Classrooms

Figure 4.1 presents a breakdown of the three configurations of pre-K classrooms in SWISD along the main dimensions of the CLASS. Our interest was in socioemotionally supportive and academically scaffolding classrooms, and the analyses of the CLASS revealed that 11 of the 36 pre-K classrooms we observed in SWISD passed muster in both regards, more or less. Specifically, what we are labeling "supportive and scaffolding" classrooms were characterized by medium-high scores in each CLASS dimension. They had high mean scores in emotional support and a near-high threshold for class-

---

1. Cluster-analytical techniques enabled this sorting of classrooms into groups based on different configurations of the three CLASS ratings in its three central domains. The k-means clustering in STATA, a partition clustering method, assigned observations to the group with the closest mean based on a predetermined number of clusters. We considered several sizes of cluster solutions and ultimately decided on a three-cluster solution, which provided the most distinct and theoretically relevant clusters while ensuring parsimony given our sample size.

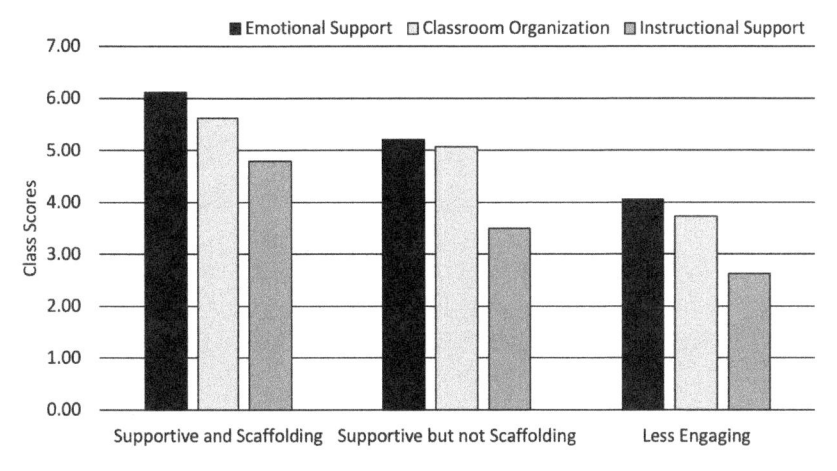

Figure 4.1. Scores by type of classroom environment

room organization, the third CLASS dimension, which we included for the sake of complementing the other two focal ones. Instructional support scores in these classrooms were in the middle of the medium range of the scale, not high in absolute terms but certainly in relative terms, well above the national average.

Beyond this focal type of early childhood education classrooms, the other two configurations tended to be lower on all classroom dimensions but in different ways. The 17 "supportive but not scaffolding" classrooms were characterized by upper-middle scores in emotional support and classroom organization, but their instructional support scores were in the low-middle range; the drop-off between their emotional support and instructional support scores was bigger than in the other configurations. In many ways, such classrooms represent the national early childhood education profile.

We labeled the third configuration as "less engaging" classrooms. These eight classrooms were in the low end of the middle range for emotional support and classroom organization, and their instructional support score was in the low range. Although instructional support reflected the national average in these classrooms, emotional support fell below most early childhood education classrooms in the country.

Notably, there was no pre-K classroom that we observed in SWISD that could be characterized as academically scaffolding in the absence of socioemotional support.

A Closer Look at Each Classroom

For more insight into this typology of early childhood education classrooms, table 4.1 presents a breakdown of the total CLASS score for each. We rely on effect sizes in standard deviation units to gauge the meaningfulness of any apparent differences across configurations. For emotional support, the difference between supportive and scaffolding classrooms and the supportive but not scaffolding classrooms (a difference equaling 0.99 of a standard deviation for all pre-K classrooms) was smaller than the difference between supportive but not scaffolding classrooms and the less engaging classrooms (1.25 SD). Classroom organization followed a similar pattern; the standard deviation difference between the supportive and scaffolding classrooms and the supportive but not scaffolding classrooms (.64 SD) was smaller than the difference between the supportive but not scaffolding classrooms and the less engaging classrooms (1.57 SD). The one exception to this general pattern was instructional support, where the former difference exceeded the latter (1.36 SD versus 0.93 SD).

Table 4.1 also presents the same information for each subdimension of each of the three CLASS dimensions. For all emotional support items, the difference between supportive but not scaffolding classrooms and the less engaging classrooms was always bigger than the difference between the supportive and scaffolding classrooms and the supportive but not scaffolding classrooms. This difference was especially strong in respect to students' perspectives and teacher sensitivity; the only exception was for positive climate, for which the two differences were virtually equal.

For classroom organization, table 4.1 reveals that this pattern (smaller differences between the first and second configurations than between the second and third) is even more consistent, especially for productivity. For instructional support, the standard deviation difference between the supportive and scaffolding classrooms and the supportive but not scaffolding classrooms was always bigger than the difference between the latter and the less engaging classrooms, especially for language modeling and quality of feedback.

Figure 4.2 presents the frequencies of each classroom configuration broken down by two other important factors. The first breakdown is by the language status of the classroom, which was defined in terms of whether instructional activities were primarily conducted in Spanish or English; the bilingual instruction classrooms were included in the former and the dual-language instruction classrooms were included in the latter along with all English-only classrooms. The second breakdown is by classroom location,

Table 4.1. Scores on CLASS dimensions and subdimensions, by classroom configuration

	\multicolumn{4}{c}{Mean (standard deviation)}			
		\multicolumn{3}{c}{Classroom type}		
	All classrooms	Supportive and scaffolding	Supportive but not scaffolding	Less engaging
Emotional support (overall)	5.22 (0.92)	6.11 (0.53)	5.20 (0.35)	4.05 (0.87)
Positive climate	5.01 (1.24)	6.52 (0.47)	4.82 (0.58)	3.13 (1.24)
Negative climate	6.21 (0.91)	6.89 (0.33)	6.18 (0.58)	5.13 (1.68)
Respect for students' perspectives	4.94 (1.06)	5.89 (0.47)	4.92 (0.76)	3.27 (0.92)
Teacher sensitivity	4.74 (1.09)	6.00 (0.50)	4.63 (0.59)	2.93 (0.55)
Classroom organization (overall)	4.94 (0.86)	5.62 (0.49)	5.07 (0.46)	3.72 (0.67)
Behavior management	4.72 (1.05)	5.69 (0.63)	4.46 (0.47)	3.14 (0.45)
Productivity	5.23 (0.76)	5.83 (0.36)	5.17 (0.44)	4.00 (0.52)
Instructional learning formats	4.88 (1.03)	5.76 (0.50)	4.73 (0.53)	3.22 (0.66)
Instructional support (overall)	3.70 (0.95)	4.79 (0.52)	3.50 (0.34)	2.62 (0.77)
Concept development	3.43 (1.03)	4.53 (0.65)	3.48 (0.55)	2.44 (0.70)
Quality of feedback	3.82 (1.20)	5.27 (0.50)	3.81 (0.53)	2.64 (0.77)
Language modeling	3.76 (0.96)	4.90 (0.49)	3.57 (0.48)	3.03 (0.75)
n	36	11	17	8

102 The Starting Line

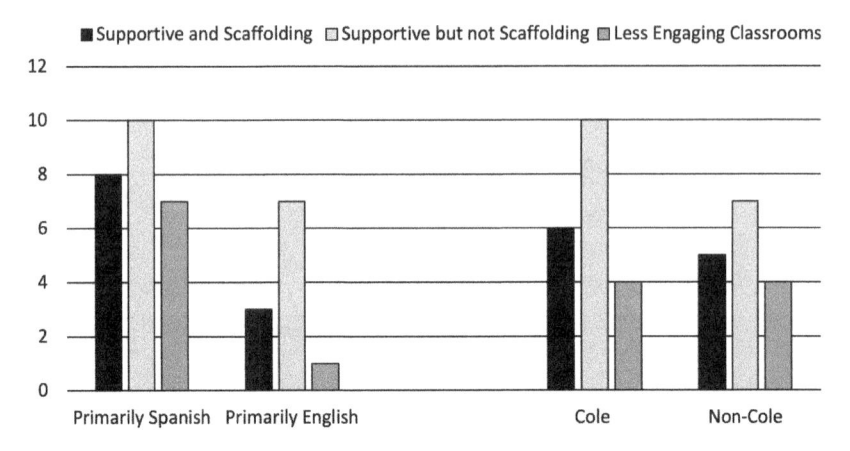

Figure 4.2. Number of classrooms in each configuration, by language and school type

which was defined by whether the classroom was at the Cole Pre-K Campus or in the home elementary school.

Primarily Spanish classrooms were overrepresented in both the supportive and scaffolding configurations and the less engaging configurations. Primarily Spanish classrooms were 69 percent of all pre-K classrooms but made up 73 percent of supportive and scaffolding classrooms and 88 percent of less engaging classrooms. Pre-K classrooms at Cole were underrepresented in the less engaging configurations. Cole classrooms made up 55 percent of all pre-K classrooms but only 50 percent of the less engaging classrooms. The big difference for Cole might be in avoiding less engaging classrooms more than housing supportive and scaffolding classrooms.

In sum, this exploration suggests that "all good things go together" in some pre-K classrooms in SWISD. Instructional support, the academic scaffolding, seemed to differentiate the various types of classrooms more than the other two categories.

Teachers in Different Kinds of Classrooms

The watching part of our time in SWISD gave us an idea of the different ways that socioemotional support and academic scaffolding could come together in early childhood education classrooms. Our parallel listening efforts provided some insight into the philosophies and strategies that help teachers link the two in their classrooms and the challenges they face in doing so. I turn now to what we learned from those conversations with teachers in the 36 pre-K classrooms in SWISD, particularly our discussions of teachers' perceptions of what makes a good classroom and how they defined success at the end of the year.

Following the mixed-methods strategy of the study, we used the three classroom configurations derived from CLASS to organize the data from our interviews with teachers. Doing so allowed us to understand how and why some classrooms appeared to be better serving the whole child. It revealed a consistent pattern in which teachers in the socioemotionally supportive and academically scaffolding classrooms were more invested than other pre-K teachers in the idea that general development and learning were deeply intertwined.

Teachers in Supportive and Scaffolding Classrooms

For teachers in classrooms that we are arguing are more in line with a developmentally appropriate concept of early childhood education quality, the primary starting point for providing an academically successful pre-K experience for young children was creating a safe and positive environment. Ms. Vargas, a pre-K teacher at the Cole Pre-K Campus, which housed several supportive and scaffolding classrooms, described what she thought was the fundamental component of a good classroom: "I would say the overall climate; [the] atmosphere of the classroom when you walk in, you can tell that there is a classroom community, where you can see that the children are happy to be at school and that [the] relationship with their teacher is a positive one and that the classroom is full of engaging activities that are meaningful for children. That to me is a good classroom."

Interestingly, although all teachers in the supportive and scaffolding classrooms said socioemotional concerns were foundational in good pre-K classrooms, they ultimately defined their own success in terms of children's acquisition of cognitive and academic skills. Ms. Rodriguez, a bilingual teacher at Cole, explained, "Success is when they show me understanding of what I'm teaching them, when they solve problems. When I assess them and they're able to explain [to] me things with more than just one word, when they elaborate, that's what makes me really feel good about myself and about teaching the students, and that's what makes me smile."

These teachers consistently expressed much higher expectations and beliefs about the academic rigor that their young students could handle than teachers did in other types of pre-K classrooms. They were also the only pre-K teachers in the sample who explicitly discussed achievement and success in terms of math, not just language and literacy. The following are examples of their statements:

> I want to just really get the ball rolling so they become learners. You know, we get this push, they're supposed to know [academic benchmarks]. They're supposed to do a lot of things for kindergarten. (Ms. Sorenson, a pre-K teacher in an elementary school)
>
> We have standards and we have to do this in order for your child [to] continue successfully into kindergarten. You know, it's learning all your letters. It's not just learning ten. Its learning all of them uppercase and lowercase, the letter sounds, putting the sounds together, and that's just scratching the surface because my kids at the end of the year, they're already reading and writing. They're writing. They're sounding out their letters, it's not perfect spelling, but what sound they hear, they're writing it down. So I tell others and they're surprised. "They're reading? They're writing?" I'm like, "Yes, why not?" (Ms. Cruz, a pre-K teacher in an elementary school)
>
> I have a few that I can say, "Wow, they've gone above and beyond." I have a few that can read, and that's true success. Some that will use [an] abacus to add and subtract, and others just guesstimate and they do pretty well. So I would say that's almost kinder[garten] and beyond, so that's true success, yeah, . . . above the requirements of preschool. (Ms. Mendez, a pre-K teacher at Cole)

One striking commonality of most teachers in the supportive and scaffolding classrooms was that they did not see the low initial academic skill level of the children entering their classrooms as a challenge. They tended to talk about that situation as an opportunity. Seeing it in a more optimistic light, they perceived more success over time. Two pre-K teachers in primarily Spanish-speaking classrooms made these observations:

> [Success is] the progress that they made. . . . They do a vocabulary assessment that looks at their real age compared to their vocabulary age at the beginning and at the end of the year, and it's always really encouraging to see the results. They make a lot more than nine months' worth of progress. It's usually [a] year and a half to three years' worth of progress in the amount of time that they're here, but that's because a lot of them started off so low. That's why we're here. (Ms. Sorensen)
>
> What I like is when I can say, "Wow, he's come so far," you know, and sometimes I forget that and somebody has to remind me that at the begin-

ning of the year that you look at him and you go, "Oh, my God," you know. At the very end of the year when you say, "Wow, he did not know a single letter when he came in." He couldn't write his name, and you know he's writing his first and his last name. He can tell you maybe not every letter, but I mean that is what success is. (Ms. Guerra)

Throughout most discussions of their pursuit of strictly academic goals, the teachers in well-rounded classrooms stood out because of their clear consideration of the developmental needs of children and meeting children where they were socially, emotionally, and psychologically to maximize their learning. Ms. Mendez emphasized that good teachers learned to cater "to every child's needs and having that patience to do so and being able to change your plans." She and many others stressed that in order to teach children reading and math, they also had to teach them classroom behavior, self-control, and self-regulation. They saw these qualities as developmentally important in general but particularly important for overcoming the academic challenges of pre-K.

In sum, teachers in supportive and scaffolding classrooms had high expectations for academic learning and pursued many challenging pedagogical strategies to fulfill these expectations. At the same time, they knew that academic challenges absent socioemotional support on the part of teachers and socioemotional maturation on the part of children would be counterproductive. They sometimes turned away from strictly academic goals in order to achieve academic gains.

Teachers in Other Types of Classrooms

The starkest contrast to the supportive and scaffolding classrooms that we observed in SWISD were the pre-K classrooms that were simultaneously low in socioemotional and instructional support. They were doubly dissimilar from the focal supportive and scaffolding classrooms in that the teachers appeared to be doing little to promote positive development, academic learning, or the interplay of the two. The teachers we interviewed who led classrooms categorized as "less engaging" by the CLASS definitions consistently emphasized the value of making their students happy in the classroom. Ms. Lozano, a pre-K teacher at Cole, remarked when asked what she thought made a good classroom, "Having students who are happy, who are happy to be here and want to learn." She went on to say, "Everything has to appeal to the students and attract them." Yet, Ms. Lozano was not often so adept at achieving these goals, and she often lost sight of academic goals in the process. In this way, she typified the teachers in the less engaging pre-K classrooms.

In many ways, the teachers in the less engaging classrooms had trouble providing supportive environments for development and learning because they saw the children as having essential deficits that needed to be fixed to learn. Especially concerning to them was what they saw as a lack of internal motivation and behavioral maturity. Ms. Rojas, a pre-K teacher at Cole, said, "They must be motivated to learn ... motivated and interested about what we're talking about because due to their age you cannot always control them. They're kids."

Such teachers tended to emphasize discipline and control rather than encouragement and scaffolding. Ms. Vasquez, a pre-K teacher in Teller Elementary, explained how to construct a good classroom by talking about what a bad classroom is: "A not-good classroom is when they don't have that, the discipline ... or when I don't have that structure. I would say classroom management, where they're not paying attention, or everybody is doing their own thing." While she and others talked about classroom quality in terms of student behavior, many other teachers talked about their end-of-year goals in terms of behavioral changes, especially in terms of self-control and obedience.

> Having self-control, that's the most important part, self-control and respect for peers and adults in school. [Interviewer: What does self-control entail?] Self-control means that you use your words and not your hands or kick or hit someone, and you need to be kind no matter what. I don't tolerate any bullying behavior or disrespect. If that's happening in my room, I call the parents immediately, and they need to stop it right there. (Ms. Arias, a pre-K teacher at Teller)
>
> My kids, when they're started, a lot of them didn't want to share, didn't know how to play together, didn't know how to communicate well with each other, or even with the teacher. So it's a lot of it you have to include within the lessons, 'This is the way that we talk.' There's a lot of hidden curriculum where it's not really in their regular curriculum. (Ms. Trujillo, a pre-K teacher at Ramirez Elementary)

Cultivating socioemotional skills like self-control, attention, and interpersonal competence were also desired goals of the supportive and scaffolding classrooms' teachers, but the difference was that the less engaging classrooms' teachers tended to pursue these goals in an overall environment that was not warm or nurturing. Moreover, these goals distracted from their academic goals rather than supporting them. Importantly, their academic expectations were quite rudimentary and entailed basic skills. None even mentioned specific reading, writing, or math skills as desired outcomes, and as illustrated by a remark from Ms. Vasquez, they viewed more advanced inferential skills as unrealistic for students with such low initial skill levels and disadvantaged backgrounds. She said, "They will have to meet the pre-K standards, so I know that if they are there then I can just add maybe more rigor, more high-order critical thinking. But if not, then my goal for the students is to just get them to at least a level where later on, when they're ready, we will be able to add up more."

The teachers in the supportive but not scaffolding classrooms were not doubly dissimilar to the teachers in the supportive and scaffolding classrooms. Like the teachers in supportive and scaffolding classrooms, they were high on many aspects of socioemotional quality. Unlike those teachers, however, they were low in the kinds of instructional quality they brought with them to the classroom. They tended to have classrooms that were warm and happy but not altogether challenging academically.

Similar to those in the less engaging classrooms, teachers in the supportive but not scaffolding classrooms emphasized creating a loving, fun, comfortable, safe, and nurturing environment that made children feel valuable. They wanted students to feel welcomed, secure, and happy. Ms. Leon, a pre-K teacher at Chavez exemplified this sentiment: "If the teacher is willing to be caring and loving and understanding and also be a strong person to where they're not going to run all over you, I think that's what makes the classroom."

In their desire to create socioemotionally positive classrooms and promote socioemotional development, however, these same teachers perhaps deemphasized academic pursuits and goals at times. They claimed to view the socioemotional components of teaching as a foundation for the academic components and indicated that challenging students and expecting much of them were essential to being good teachers. Teachers in pre-K classrooms on and off the Cole Pre-K Campus made these comments:

> And then at the end of the year I would say that it's successful if my children are ready for kindergarten. They understand procedures, they are ready to read, writing the letters, the numbers, you know. They know the colors without even thinking twice, they're starting to spell out words, invent words, and they're writing. They really need to be writing. (Ms. Wallace, at Teller)
>
> What really makes a good classroom is clear, consistent expectations.

I would also add high expectations. We really stress independence in our children. (Ms. Harris, at Cole)

A good classroom is when you know your students and you know the needs they have, you can build your curriculum, your assessments, your daily routines to them. (Ms. Medina, at Cole)

Yet teachers in these supportive but not scaffolding classrooms often did not follow through on their academic goals, even as they strove to facilitate the positive development of their young students. Sometimes those goals proved hard to reach, and so they seemed to find solace in other successes. Ms. Munoz, a pre-K teacher at Ramirez Elementary, explained, "Basically at the end of the day you know if they have gotten the concept or not . . . also if they're engaged, if you see that they're having fun, and that's to me the most important thing, that they're engaged in doing something that they're enjoying."

Another striking characteristic of the pre-K teachers in the supportive but not scaffolding classrooms in SWISD was that they tended to view themselves as achieving a great deal of academic success even when our observational ratings suggested that little cognitively stimulating activity or advanced skill-building was going on in their classrooms. We heard from one generally low-rated pre-K teacher at Cole,

I always have bright students. They're always able to do more than I anticipated because the perception of pre-K. They are seriously capable of a super-high level. I mean, look at my window [with their work posted]. I'm having them doing addition, and they understand exactly what they're doing. They understand how to add it together; they're writing their addition down. So I think a rigorous, obviously a rigorous classroom, it's a good sign, . . . a rigorous, controlled, positive, loving, organized classroom, because you know things like boundaries and organization are something that a child doesn't know that they need, but they're searching for that. I always have all students at almost all fours [perfect score] in their report cards.

The teachers in the supportive but not scaffolding classrooms were certainly doing more for their children in terms of socioemotional development and academic learning than teachers in the less engaging classrooms, but they had more to do to cultivate the interplay between the two at the heart of developmentally appropriate practices. They were not serving the whole child.

A False Dichotomy

False dichotomies of early childhood education are obstacles to serving young children from low-income Latina/o families. Those false dichotomies could take the form of a perceived separation between early childhood education and elementary school or an assumed boundary between learning at home and learning at school. To that list can be added the false dichotomy of social and emotional development being separate from cognitive and academic development as focal goals of early childhood education and efforts to foster each as core processes of early childhood education.

There is a lingering belief among many that an emphasis on socioemotional development represents a dilution of the academic gains to be had from enrolling children in early childhood education. There is also concern that a more academic emphasis might crowd out opportunities for children's social and emotional development (Fuller et al., 2017; Le et al., 2019). That these tensions tend to be especially felt in Latina/o communities and the schools serving them calls for a culturally grounded educational approach for the children and families being served. Classrooms that provide a socioemotionally supportive and academically scaffolding environment for the young children of low-income Latina/o parents reflect this spirit of cultural grounding. They can do so by balancing the different ways that families and educators may approach the complexities of early learning and by integrating parental values of the importance of raising well-behaved and academically successful children.

A considerable number of pre-K classrooms in SWISD could be characterized as socioemotionally supportive and academically scaffolding environments for young children, and only a small minority of pre-K classrooms that we observed in the district could be characterized as lacking either ingredient of high-quality education. Within this general distinction between "All good things go together" and "Bad in one way is bad in all ways" are more specific patterns:

- Elements of academic scaffolding, especially those related to the cultivation of critical thinking skills and higher-order thought processes, are the weak links in early childhood education, generally lagging behind other components of classroom quality.
- Although there were classrooms that tilted toward socioemotional support more than academic scaffolding, there were none that tilted the other way; socioemotional support was possible in the absence of academic scaf-

folding, but academic scaffolding was virtually nonexistent without socioemotional support.
- Teachers' respect for children's perspectives and their modeling of language in the classroom were two particular classroom processes that set socioemotionally supportive and academically scaffolding classrooms apart from others.
- Although the classrooms we observed were predominantly populated by Latina/o children, those operating primarily in Spanish tended to most reflect the "All good things go together" pattern in that they were more likely to feature both or neither socioemotional support and academic scaffolding rather than some combination of the two.
- The Cole Pre-K Campus had, in raw terms, more socioemotionally supportive and academically scaffolding classrooms and fewer less engaging classrooms than the traditional elementary schools, suggesting that this all-preschool organizational arrangement was better at fostering socioemotionally supportive early education regardless of the academic nature of instruction.
- Teachers in socioemotionally supportive and academically scaffolding classrooms were guided first and foremost by academic goals and judged themselves accordingly, but they said socioemotionally supportive practices helped them reach these goals, especially when the children faced academic challenges.
- Other teachers tended to elevate behavioral or socioemotional goals as their desired outcomes and appeared to have a less clear sense of themselves as teachers in terms of their everyday classroom practices and experiences.

The needs and strengths of very young children being introduced to formal education are about all of the cognitive and academic skills they can acquire as a foundation for future educational pursuits but also the social and emotional skills they will use to engage with and navigate the educational system. Meeting those needs and capitalizing on those strengths requires a culturally grounded approach that recognizes where young children and their parents are coming from and ensures that the school is respecting their beliefs and values. The pre-K classrooms in SWISD that we characterized as socioemotionally supportive and academically scaffolding were the best equipped to meet children's needs and capitalize on their strengths, and the teachers leading these classrooms seemed to be best equipped to work with students and their families in culturally grounded ways. They were well positioned to bridge the false dichotomies of early childhood education.

CHAPTER 5

Connecting Needs and Challenges

Another way to connect the within-classroom processes of early childhood education programs serving young children from low-income Latina/o families is to consider how they balance the competing academic needs of diverse groups of children in day-to-day educational activities. In exploring this cross-activity balance within classrooms, my focus is on one key subset of the large and heterogeneous population of Latina/o children: English language learners. Such children, who also are often referred to as "dual language learners," are learning English in addition to their or their parents' native language. Achieving bilingualism has great cognitive, social, and economic benefits, but it is also difficult, especially in a US educational system that is decidedly monolingual. Indeed, the system is organized around English language instruction and English-only materials and curricula. As a result, English language learners might face barriers to learning and skill development as they attempt to achieve bilingualism. Thus, even though bilingualism ultimately will be an advantage, the process of becoming bilingual can be a disadvantage in the short term. This disadvantage, in turn, can often mean that the native language is dropped while English is adopted, switching one type of monolingualism for another (Takanishi & Le Menestrel, 2017). A long-standing challenge for US schools, therefore, is to help English language learners realize the advantages of bilingualism while buffering them against disadvantages along the way. That challenge is particularly acute in early childhood education, which often marks the first broad exposure to English for children from low-income immigrant families. Efforts to meet this challenge can be supported by identifying and understanding the pitfalls along the way.

Aida Ramos collaborated with me on this chapter.

My purpose in this chapter is to examine that understanding of the pitfalls. It is organized by two concepts from educational research and practice. "Instructional demand" refers to the pressures on teachers to pursue many tasks and goals in a relatively limited amount of time. These pressures create a zero-sum game, with attention to one thing leading to inattention to another. "Counterfeit social capital" refers to a shallow form of social support from teachers who are less concerned with improving the academic outcomes of Latina/o students and more concerned with managing their classrooms, instructional activities, and self-concepts as effective teachers (Ream, 2003; Stanton-Salazar, 2001).

Both concepts emphasize how teachers often unknowingly and unintentionally shortchange the children who deserve the most investment. Teachers want their students to succeed and work actively to serve them, but the often overwhelming daily circumstances of their jobs means that they do so in ways that might not actually help students succeed in the long run. Some teachers with large proportions of English language learners in their classrooms seem to react to the challenges of teaching English and academic skills at the same time by emphasizing their role in helping English language learners develop socioemotional skills instead. The children derive some benefits from this approach, but they fall behind other children, including other Latina/o children, in building academic foundations for elementary school. Elucidating how practical realities undermine the goals of well-meaning teachers can lead to figuring out how to address those practical realities.

For this chapter, that elucidation uses our SWISD experiences to identify differences in teachers' perceptions of the factors that undermine and support daily instructional activities in classrooms. Some of these classrooms are populated by Latina/o English language learners, and others are not. Comparing the two sets of classrooms provides an on-the-ground glimpse into a timely discussion of educational policy and practice targeting a timely demographic issue, that of just what young Latina/o children from low-income families are being taught at the starting line.

Language-Related Disparities in Education

The dramatic growth of the English language learner population in recent decades, largely as a result of immigration and births to immigrants, has been the focus of a great deal of educational policy and practice. About 10 percent of students in US schools are labeled English language learners, meaning that they are viewed as needing to develop sufficient English skills to actively engage in English language classrooms. This proportion is much higher in Texas, at nearly 17 percent in 2016, and nationally is growing rapidly and likely to double or even triple in the coming years. Tellingly, kindergarten and the primary grades house far greater percentages of English language learners than later grades; previous generations of English language learners are now being replaced by even larger generations. Although English language learners come from diverse backgrounds, immigration histories, and family language use, the overwhelming majority are Spanish-speaking children of Latin American immigrants (Calderón et al., 2011; Hopper, 2012; National Center for Education Statistics, 2018).

The debates that have been generated by the growth of the Latina/o English language learner population are rooted in the well-documented achievement disparities between English language learners and their peers. The former consistently have lower achievement test scores and grades in elementary school, a disparity that grows as they progress through school and then translates into lower educational attainment (Goldenberg 2008; Takanishi & Le Menestrel, 2017). Consequently, English language learner status is one of the categories for government-mandated disaggregation of test score reporting, meaning that a school has to provide results of testing specifically for this group of students when reporting its overall achievement. That disaggregation is intended to shine a light on inequalities among diverse student groups (Lauen & Gaddis, 2012).

The general argument about the value of early childhood education for reducing socioeconomic and demographic disparities in academic achievement and educational attainment (Heckman, 2006) is particularly relevant to children from immigrant families, especially English language learners. This heightened value is seen in the design of numerous programs attempting to boost the early educational experiences of children in this population to prepare them and their families for the US educational system; among them are Avance, Abriendo Puertas, and Project FLAME (Family Literacy—Aprendiendo, Mejorando, Educando) (Crosnoe, 2010). It is also why several state-funded public pre-K programs have targeted this group of Latina/o children. Oklahoma's universal pre-K initiative has been noted for its apparent success in improving the academic outcomes of Latina/o English language learners, and the Texas pre-K initiative explicitly endorses English language learner status as one of its eligibility criteria (Andrews et al., 2012; Chang et al., 2007; Gormley et al., 2005).

With the growing enrollment of Latina/o English language learners in early childhood education programs and the apparently favorable results of their enrollment, more attention is being paid to the instructional learning activities within the pre-K programs that are serving this population (Fuller, 2007; Karoly & Gonzalez, 2011). Such inquiry involves breaking down pre-K classrooms into their basic elements of instructional practices and interpersonal interactions to understand the potential resources to build on and concerns to address. In this spirit, I decided to focus on classroom processes that might shed light on one enduring vulnerability of Latina/o English language learners in the K-12 system that might also undermine the effectiveness of early childhood education. That vulnerability is the potential extra challenge of teaching English language learners, which increases the challenges of teaching children substantive subject matter more generally (Cho & Reich, 2008). I do so by considering challenges as perceived by teachers. Teachers' perceptions of their professional ups and downs likely shape how they construct and follow through on their pedagogical goals and, in turn, how effectively they meet the needs of English language learners.

With this focus on teacher perceptions, I fully recognize that any person's perceptions, including my own, can be biased or inaccurate. Yet, in line with the Thomas theorem (Thomas & Thomas, 1928) that something is real if its consequences are real, even biased and inaccurate perceptions held by teachers can have very real implications for the young children in their care. A teacher may hold class- or ethnic-based prejudices about student ability that lead to lower estimations of a child's academic skills, resulting in decreased instructional investment in that child that eventually deflates his or her achievement. The perception is wrong, but the consequences are real. On the flip side, teachers' perceptions may also reflect the reality of their classrooms and the potential of the children in them. In both cases, teachers' perceptions are a meaningful barometer of the pre-K experiences of Latina/o English language learners (Tobin et al., 2013).

Perceived Instructional Challenges

When I consider challenges to the academic instruction in pre-K classrooms with Latina/o English language learners, I am referring to obstacles blocking the degree to which teachers are able to set up, work through, and support classroom-based activities and interactions that build critical thinking skills. Those skills require and expand high-order cognitive functioning such as interpretation, analysis, and generalization, and are crucial for children to develop early if they are to reach their academic potential in formal schooling (Pianta, Belsky, Houts, et al. 2007). How well critical skills are being

Figure 5.1 diagram:
- A Priori Risks: Time Constraints, Perceived Instruction Fit, Compensation
- + Emergent Risks ?
- → Disrupted Skill-Building Instruction for English Language Learners

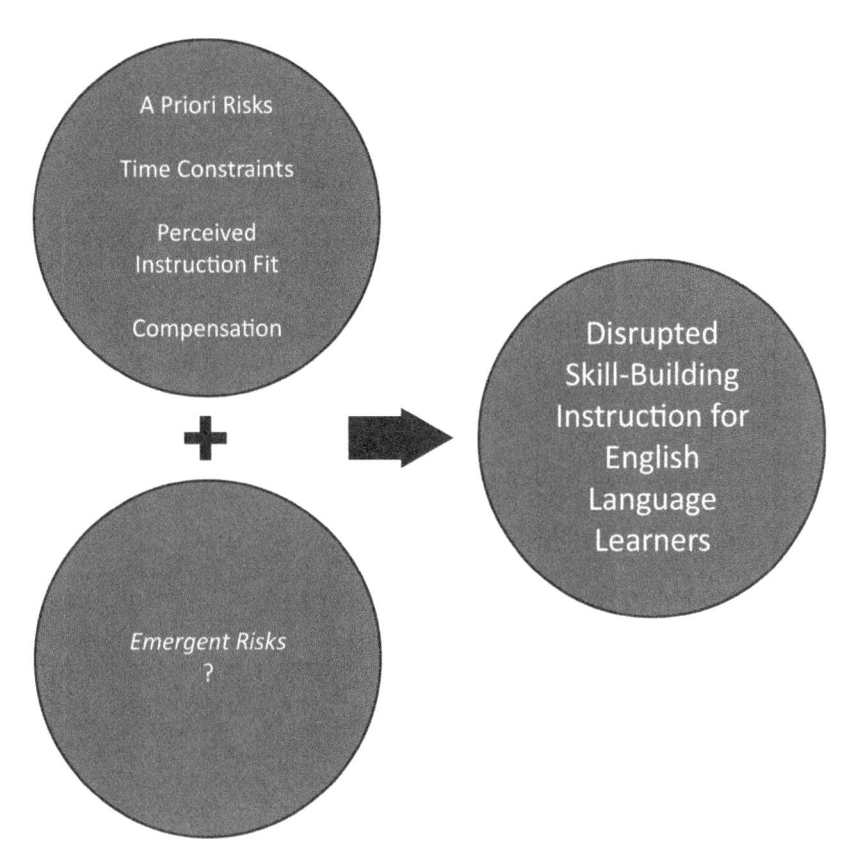

Figure 5.1. Perceived risks to instruction in higher-order cognitive and academic skills

developed is a key element of the long-term effectiveness of early childhood education.

Figure 5.1 presents a model of risk factors, as perceived by teachers, in their ability to facilitate this kind of learning and development in those classrooms relative to pre-K classrooms without Latina/o English language learners. Here, "risk factors" refers to classroom processes that reduce the probability of children in that classroom receiving instruction to build such skills. Some classrooms may feature these processes and still maintain high levels of that kind of instruction, but the term "risk" means this scenario has lower odds of happening when compared to a classroom without those same processes. For the purposes of our research and in line with the grounded theory approach of the study (Charmaz, 2006), these risk factors are broken down into two categories that draw on the language of grounded theory already discussed: the processes that I expected to see in classrooms and hear from teachers based on past research and theory, "a priori" risks (Calderón et al., 2011; Goldenberg, 2008), and the "emergent" classroom processes that I came to see as relevant through such discussions with teachers and observations of classrooms (Ryan & Bernard, 2003).

Classroom Realities

So, what did I expect to see and hear? The first answer to this question is based on my acute awareness that being a teacher of young children is quite difficult in general and especially in this climate of ever higher standards for school performance without commensurate resources and support. Much is demanded of teachers regardless of who their students are, and the day rarely seems long enough to meet those demands. If time is a constraint, something will get lost. That is true of any classroom, but it is especially true in a classroom filled with students who have instructional needs that go beyond standard academic goals. A classroom with large numbers of English language learners is a good example of that scenario, when a teacher is tasked with helping children learn English while also engaging in the other expected instructional activities.

Teachers in classrooms with English language learners have additional instructional tasks that other teachers do not have, although they have the same amount of instructional time in the day. They must work on cultivating English proficiency in addition to core instructional tasks, both basic ones, such as teaching numbers, and higher order ones, such as facilitating interpretative skills, while other teachers have only to focus on the core tasks (Gándara et al., 2005). Balancing those needs is crucial to the overall academic development of English language learners and whether they reach grade-level skills and proficiencies. Evidence suggests that when teachers systematically couple skill-focused instructional content with sheltered English language instruction (integrating language and content-based instruction in the same learning activities), English language learners tend to perform better on academic tasks and assessments than English language learners who do not receive the same mix in their classrooms. Achieving this balance in the classroom requires careful planning, adequate class time, and pedagogical flexibility (Echevarría et al., 2006; Gándara et al., 2005; Goldenberg, 2008).

As another practical matter, most federal and state legislation does not require that teachers who have many English language learners in their classrooms gain additional training in instructional methods for this specific population of children. Such methods could include sheltered language teaching or secondary language acquisition. As a result of lacking a requirement, there has been a shortage of teachers with sufficient training to effectively address the language needs of students even as the numbers of such students have grown (Echevarría et al., 2006; Takanishi & Le Menestrel, 2017).

Exacerbating this challenge are structural constraints. Schools with large numbers of English language learners are more likely to face resource shortfalls that limit their ability to assist teachers with managing their workloads; they also are more likely to hire teachers with minimal qualifications (de Cohen & Clewell, 2007; Fry, 2011; Solórzano, 2008). Thus, the instructional demands of early childhood education for English language learners may dilute the degree of cognitive stimulation and scaffolding that teachers provide to such students, regardless of their intent or goals.

Classroom Trade-Offs

Another answer to the question of what I expected to see and hear is based on my understanding of the human tendency to develop explanations for events that justify one's course of action, including by attributing the cause of some difficult situation to external circumstances (Mezulis et al., 2004). Basically, when there is a possibility that people will be judged by themselves or others for some disappointing outcome, they search for complex rather than simplistic answers to buffer them from blame. This human tendency does not mean that these explanations are always wrong, but it does mean that people sometimes engage in thinking and acting to provide clarity to themselves and others that is not easy to come by.

Teachers who do not engage in as much cognitively stimulating activity in classrooms with English language learners than they otherwise would might see that as a function of instructional fit. They could shy away from more challenging instruction and learning activities because they believe students are not ready to tackle them for what they see as substantial barriers to meeting those challenges. The role of teacher expectations is complicated when children enter educational settings with varied levels of academic preparedness because of differences in life circumstances in developmental domains such as their health and psychological development and in contexts such as their family situations and whether they had early child care outside their homes (Crosnoe et al., 2015; Genishi & Dyson, 2009; Tobin et al., 2013). Low levels of experience with English are certainly likely to be seen by at least some teachers as a barrier to tackling challenging instruction and learning activities. That perception can also be colored by other factors such as family poverty and parents who do not speak English; those factors also tend to be more common among Latina/o English language learners (Fuller, 2007; Crosnoe, 2006).

Teacher assessments of children are not just what they think students can handle but also what they think students will get at home in terms of active scaffolding and support (Arias & Morillo-Campbell, 2008; Gándara et al., 2005; Karabenick & Noda, 2004; Ramirez, 2003). If teachers think that English language learners have only rudimentary academic skills, that they need attention to other areas of development such as self-regulation, and that their parents may not be able to help them, the teachers may perceive that shifting time away from content-focused instructional activity such as literacy and quantitative thinking and toward more basic skill development such as recognizing words and numbers is the right course of action (Gándara et al., 2005). Thus, teachers organize their activities according to what they think their students need, and their perceptions of need may be colored by children's and parents' facility with English skills. These perceptions may also reinforce and be reinforced by what is already happening in their classrooms; in other words, teachers engage in classroom activities with students, and these activities then color how teachers retroactively and prospectively think about the motivations and reasons for engaging in them.

As another example, compensation is a variant on perceived instructional fit. Teachers of English language learners deal with the challenges of their pedagogical mission by playing up other aspects of teacher-student interactions. They may strive for different kinds of development besides content-focused instruction to promote the development of higher-order cognitive skills. This potential risk is seen in research on Latina/o students in secondary schools that has shown how teachers engage in instructional activities with good intentions of helping students but ultimately sell them short (Ream, 2003; Villenas & Foley, 2002). Teachers may think they are helping Latina/o students achieve success in life by downplaying their development of academic skills or doing less to create academic opportunities for them while prioritizing classroom harmony, socioemotional support, and socialization. They face an arena that is challenging to them by identifying other arenas of success.

Early childhood education teachers in classrooms with English language learners might place more emphasis on building socioemotional skills than cognitive skills as a form of coping. Some overwhelmed teachers may give their students what they convince themselves is really important for students' futures. They see it as offering students valuable social capital to help them get ahead, but that capital might not prove to be so valuable in the long term if not coupled with a strong academic foundation; hence comes the term "counterfeit social capital."

Other Classroom Issues

Turning from a priori to emergent risk factors, I cast a wide net over the qualitative (listening) data by considering a broad array of teachers' experiences in and out of early childhood education classrooms with children, parents, fellow teachers, and administrators. I also considered common characteristics and circumstances of English language learners and their families such as race/ethnicity and socioeconomic status that could magnify or mask teachers' perceptions of teaching English language learners, including in terms of the three a priori risk factors already described. Basically, I had good reason for thinking that I would see and hear some revealing comments about teachers' perceptions, but I did not want to be limited by my expectations.

A Picture of Classroom Instruction in SWISD

Our two methods of collecting data, watching and talking, in SWISD are relevant to understanding the specific case of cognitively stimulating instruction for young Latina/o English language learners; we drew on both to explore the a priori expectations about the perceived challenges and go in more unexpected directions with my exploration. This time, however, I narrowed the range of interest to two years in the PK-3 window instead of four, the pre-K year and the kindergarten year. That choice reflected the special vulnerability of English language learners during the transition into elementary school and concerns about consistency and progression in learning activities across this transition.

To that end, Aida and I looked at the data from the 44 classrooms in these two grade levels. Of them, 30 classrooms (25 pre-K and 5 kindergarten) were characterized by significant instructional support for English language learners, so we refer to them as primarily Spanish classrooms. The remaining 14 classrooms (11 pre-K and 3 kindergarten, including some with the dual language format) did not have any form of support, and the teachers in these classrooms reported that they had no English language learners as students; we refer to them as English classrooms. The students in the primarily Spanish classrooms were almost entirely Latina/o, and most were first- or second-generation Mexican American. About two-thirds of the student population in these 44 pre-K and kindergarten classrooms were Latina/o children; those proportions were in keeping with the composition of the SWISD student population as a whole. We were mostly comparing children who shared an ethnic background but differed in their language status. Similarly, 28 of the 44 teachers were Latinas, with a higher proportion of Latina teachers in the subsample of primarily Spanish classrooms.

Looking for Cognitively Stimulating Instructional Activities

Key to this exploration is the importance of cognitively stimulating instruction to help children develop critical thinking skills. CLASS proved quite valuable in assessing what was going on inside classrooms and comparing one classroom to another. The teacher activities and teacher-student interactions that CLASS observers are cued to look for in classrooms under the umbrella category of instructional support, as one of the three main dimensions of CLASS, were most relevant to this concept of cognitively stimulating instruction. Instructional support is broken up into subdimensions with different focal processes, such as the following:

- *Concept development* through analysis and reasoning, creation, integration, and connection to the real world;
- *Quality of feedback* through scaffolding, feedback loops, promoting through processes, providing information, and encouragement and affirmation;
- *Language modeling* through frequent conversation, open-ended questions, repetition and extension, self- and parallel talk, and advanced language.

Given my interest in classrooms serving large numbers of English language learners, I also wanted to conduct an observational assessment specific to bilingual instruction. My original plan was to conduct the Sheltered Instruction Observation Protocol (SIOP) alongside CLASS in classrooms with English language learners that involved Spanish-language instruction (Echevarría et al., 2006).

Spanish-language instruction was so pervasive and English instruction or really just English usage so rare in most of the classrooms serving English language learners that the SIOP proved to be difficult if not impossible to field in all but a few classrooms. The problems we had with the SIOP suggest how much of a misnomer "bilingual instruction" was in pre-K and kindergarten classrooms in SWISD. My guess is that SWISD is less the exception than the rule in this regard.

Table 5.1. Mean CLASS scores for instructional support, by grade level and classroom language instruction

		Mean (standard deviation)			
		Pre-K		*Kindergarten*	
	All	*Spanish*	*English*	*Spanish*	*English*
Main domain rating					
Instructional support	3.75	3.54	4.06	3.86	4.26
	(1.01)	(.99)	(.80)	(1.42)	(1.58)
Items within main domain					
Concept development	3.54	3.28	3.76	3.93	4.22
	(1.17)	(1.03)	(1.00)	(1.88)	(1.64)
Quality of feedback	3.86	3.63	4.27	3.93	4.22
	(1.22)	(1.26)	(.93)	(1.44)	(1.68)
Language modeling	3.77	3.59	4.15	3.47	4.33
	(1.01)	(.99)	(.79)	(1.19)	(1.53)
n	44	25	11	5	3

Seeing Cognitively Stimulating Instructional Activities

Table 5.1 presents a breakdown of the CLASS dimension most aligned with our focus on instruction aiming to develop critical thinking, that is, instructional support. Starting with pre-K, the primarily Spanish and primarily English classrooms differed in their average instructional support ratings. The mean of concept development for primarily Spanish classrooms (3.28) was 0.48 lower than the mean for the primarily English classrooms (3.76). Likewise, the former had lower means than the latter on quality of feedback (primarily English classrooms – primarily Spanish classrooms = 0.64) and language modeling (primarily English classrooms – primarily Spanish classrooms = 0.56). When these three subscales were combined into a total score for instructional support, the disparity between primarily Spanish and primarily English classrooms, favoring the latter, was 0.52.

I use standard deviations to describe effect sizes, with a difference of between one quarter and one half a standard deviation considered to be a moderate effect and anything above that considered to be large. The effect sizes for the differences just described were 40 percent of a standard deviation (*SD*) for concept development, 52 percent *SD* for quality of feedback, 55 percent *SD* for language modeling, and 51 percent *SD* for the total instructional support scale combining the first three. By conventional standards, these effect sizes are moderate to large. Thus, primarily Spanish pre-K classrooms seemed to involve less stimulating and skill-building instruction than primarily English classrooms.

Turning to the far smaller sample from kindergarten, primarily Spanish classrooms were rated lower than primarily English classrooms on all three subscales of instructional support. The effect sizes ranged from 25 percent *SD* for concept development, 24 percent *SD* for quality of feedback, and 85 percent *SD* for language modeling. The effect size for the full instructional support scale was 40 percent *SD*.

In sum, primarily Spanish and primarily English pre-K and kindergarten classrooms appeared to differ in the CLASS domain that best taps into cognitively stimulating and skill-building instruction. This disparity was somewhat less pronounced in size of effect in the small subsample of kindergarten classrooms than in the larger census of pre-K classrooms.

Hearing from Teachers in SWISD

With this background from the CLASS observations, interviews with teachers can identify and elucidate potential disruptions to cognitively stimulating instructional processes in pre-K and kindergarten, with special attention to perceived challenges that were more difficult for teachers in primarily Spanish classrooms. These interviews with the teachers in the same 44 classrooms in which we conducted the CLASS offered them an opportunity to articulate the challenges they encountered when teaching pre-K and kindergarten, including for English language learners. They provided a rich account of the underlying risk factors that could be affecting cognitively stimulating instructional processes that would otherwise be unknown or captured in much less depth in the CLASS. One segment of the interviews focused on the rewards and challenges perceived by teachers specific to the predominant child group in the classroom, low-income children in general and/or English language learners, and their experiences with the school and larger district related to both rewards and challenges. That section is the most relevant to this chapter and provided much of the insight described here.

As a preview, Aida and I identified three key challenges that could be characterized as hybrids of the categories of a priori and emergent risk factors. One challenge was confined to the primarily Spanish classrooms, and two were more general but appeared to be heightened in primarily Spanish classrooms. The sections below describe these challenges, drawing on the narratives of individual teachers to illustrate the collective themes that arose across all interviews. Worth stressing is that these three challenges are not mutually exclusive. Teachers who experienced one type of challenge typically faced others; we found this especially among teachers in primarily Spanish pre-K classrooms. I should also reiterate that some teacher perceptions are likely to be accurate and objective, while some are likely to be biased and inaccurate, although all perceptions matter to children to the extent that they shape teachers' behavior in the classroom.

Literacy Challenges

Nearly all pre-K teachers in primarily Spanish classrooms articulated how less-developed English skills among their students posed problems to the task of helping children become academically school ready (in pre-K) or prepared for the primary grades (in kindergarten). Ms. Sorenson, a white pre-K teacher, noted, "I get some students and I feel like they're eighteen months old. They don't have toileting skills. I've had kids that they just grunt, and then I have kids who are slightly reading when they walk in the door. It's all over the place."

A Latina pre-K teacher in a primarily Spanish classroom in a different school, Ms. Muñoz, expressed the same sentiment: "Their language in both English and Spanish is very limited, so when we get them in pre-K we basically get them with no language. Actually, they're very limited in Spanish and in English, . . . and that's the biggest challenge."

Many teachers in primarily Spanish classrooms expressed some frustration over the difficulty of traversing the various language challenges while trying to instruct children in school curricula. Ms. Mendez, a Latina teacher at Cole, mentioned the impact on general instruction of having children with underdeveloped English skills: "In terms of the different levels that they do come in [with,] . . . the backgrounds that they do have, it makes it challenging, yes. Because I do have to strategize and sort of custom-make the lecture or objective that I'm trying to get across towards different level children."

During a fast-paced day, taking the time to address the language needs of students made it more difficult for teachers to focus on content. Ms. Mendez discussed the additional work she put into her lesson plans to make content objectives accessible across students' various language levels. This discussion was similar to what Ms. Villareal, a Latina pre-K teacher on site in an elementary school, described: "Well, you know, it's challenging for me because the students in this particular class, since their dominant language is Spanish and so . . . it's hard for me not to want to translate to Spanish to make it just easier for them. I've had to definitely work at that and try to use more context clues, pictures, and graphics and everything possible . . . so I stay in the language of instruction of the day."

The increase in curriculum-dictated pre-K content calling for language literacy was seen as a challenge to instruction when combined with the less-developed vocabulary for English language learners. Another first-year bilingual pre-K teacher, Ms. Rodriguez at Cole, shared this observation:

My students arrive at school with a very low vocabulary on average. . . . [Interviewer: Do you have any idea why?] Because they [the parents] don't talk to them. Everything is called this, that, or the other, 'Bring me this, bring me that, sit here, sit there.' Nothing has a name. So it's hard for students to talk like that if they're exposed to these types of situations at home or with their relatives. So that's a big challenge I have to fight every year. . . . You ask them, "Bring me . . . or Where's my notebook?" [and] all of them will point. The first reaction they have is to just point. . . . They'll walk to where it is, but they would not tell you what it is.

Teachers suggested that children's lack of vocabulary had a direct impact on phonics instruction, and they noted its connection to the increasing demand for literacy skills by schools for each grade. Ms. Muñoz, who was formerly a kindergarten teacher, pointed out, "As a kinder[garten] teacher, what I would tell a pre-K teacher is that because of us becoming more like first grade or kinder becoming more like first grade, it would help if they knew their letters and sounds, definitely all of them, and in Spanish, the syllables because that is when they start to read."

Often, these teachers blurred the lines between English skills and general literacy. Their perception was that the skill levels of students were not a good match with their own instructional goals or the goals imposed by the district. Overall, teachers said the language issues of English language learners affected what the teachers could do and undermined one-on-one instruction. They also directly connected what was going on with children to their parents' own language backgrounds. Thus, language-related challenges added to the general instructional challenges of early education.

Socioeconomic Challenges

Most public early childhood education programs were created to serve low-income communities, a target that increasingly encompasses English language learners especially in a state like Texas. Despite this reality, the SWISD teachers expressed dismay over the more disadvantaged socioeconomic backgrounds of their students, even more so in primarily Spanish classrooms. Ms. Vasquez, a Latina pre-K teacher in a primarily Spanish classroom, explained,

> I have some students that the background that they brought with them, the knowledge that they brought with them was already high and since the beginning, and I was just adding up to what they already know. So I had to keep the lessons challenging for them, but then I had to also go down to the level of my other ones who didn't even know the letters. So that was at the beginning. It was kind of challenging for my lessons to divide them into groups.

Ms. Sorenson shared a similar sentiment: "I think it makes instruction harder because my classroom doesn't necessarily represent what the future classrooms will be in the school. You have to be economically disadvantaged to qualify for my school [Cole] or for my classroom to be in the pre-K program, and I do think there are more challenges for those kids starting off."

Teachers tended to view the largely disadvantaged socioeconomic backgrounds of their students as a liability that needed to be overcome, as expressed by another Latina pre-K teacher, Ms. Rojas at Cole: "And, unfortunately, in this type of bilingual class, we get children with very low backgrounds. Very low because due to the same problems of which we all know about, . . . the low educational background that the family has and all that."

Additionally, teachers in some more diverse schools equated the socioeconomic variation they saw in their classrooms to behavioral problems among children who interrupted instructional activities. Ms. Kellerman, a white kindergarten teacher with a more socioeconomically diverse classroom than in the pre-K program overall, recounted,

> I have kids whose parents are both lawyers and a bunch of kids who are low SES [socioeconomic status]. And that makes it an interesting mix, and I would say that more than culture has an effect on the classroom. As a teacher

you don't want to let anybody down, but when there's a student who really has no self-control and is interrupting up the class instruction all the time, you have to look for strategies to deal with them but also keep all these other kids engaged and working on something.

This issue is connected to teachers' perceptions of the cultural capital—the knowledge and experiences that suggest status to others—of children from Latina/o language minority families. Ms. Arias, a Latina pre-K teacher, explained that she noticed the various differences in children's lives outside of school by socioeconomic status:

> I have low-income students, middle-class, middle-high-class, and professional parents.... The environment is completely different from one to the other, and usually the students have come from social economical levels higher than the ones from [a housing project]. They have background knowledge, very rich. The others don't have any at all. So it was really hard to level that, even in the social skills and some emotional interaction between them. ... The other students that come from low SES and families, poverty culture, ... it's very damaging for the academic part of the development of the student and the academic part because they come with no tools, so they have to build the tools in schools in order to be successful.

Partly, teachers attributed this perceived lack of cultural capital among their students to those students' parents. An example is found in an earlier, telling quote from a white teacher in a dual-language instruction school, Ms. Kellerman at Teller: "I've been exposed to the zoo, and I've been exposed to, you know, all kinds of different places, and I go out and I hike every weekend, and I, as opposed to a lot of, unfortunately, the low-SES students, [who] go home and watch TV all evening or go home and play video games all weekend."

Teachers' perceptions of the lack of cultural capital of Latina/o English language learners translated, in their view, into direct problems for instruction. Ms. Denton, a white kindergarten teacher with a primarily Spanish classroom, recalled,

> I'm doing this reading lesson on real structured phonics, and it has words in there that are three letters that the kids from lower economic groups don't know what they mean. You know, like, "cot." "What's a cot?" ... These are short words everybody knows what these mean, but they don't know these words, so they read things and you think this is an easy little sentence, but it

doesn't have any meaning to them.... So you're trying to build those little tiny things to get them to read.

Overall, teachers perceived "deficits" (problem behavior, lack of cultural capital) that were assumed to go along with students' family circumstances, especially in socioeconomically mixed classrooms. In these circumstances, the teachers were frustrated that they had to work on knowledge that they thought students should already have, putting them behind in core instructional activities. They thought the socioeconomic disadvantages that tended to co-occur with English language learner status in this district represented another add-on to the general challenges of teaching young children.

Parent-Related Challenges

Substantially overlapping with the discussion of family-school-community partnerships, a common theme of our time in SWISD was that teachers perceived parents to be a challenge in their jobs rather than a support. This perception was strongest when teachers had students from low-income language-minority families, and it undoubtedly affected the classroom efficacy of teachers. For the most part, teachers who were concerned about the parents of children in primarily Spanish classrooms said the parents were distant or did not understand the demands of US schooling. Ms. Castro, a white pre-K teacher, describes her view: "They don't really come into the classroom. They don't do tutoring; they don't do anything like that.... I don't know if other grades have parents actually working with kids, but I haven't really observed that." Ms. Fernandez said, "I mean, the parents try, but their responses, out of seventeen children, I'll get homework back from seven.... I have to constantly be calling and training them.... On Sundays I come sometimes and train some of the parents so that they know what to do.... There's some skills that we do here that if the parent doesn't do it at home, there's no way we can do it."

The teachers' responsive strategies were communication-based. Ms. Rivera, a Latina bilingual kindergarten teacher, said, "I also stress, 'Please read to your child every night,' if they can, 'cause I also send like little emergent books with them so that they can read this at home every day. I really emphasize to them, just help them because it's mostly what we did the week before, ... and they need to reinforce some of the skills that we have had [in the classroom]."

When we probed further, SWISD teachers typically explained what they saw as low involvement in terms of the unstable work schedules and low incomes of the parents of Spanish-speaking students. Ms. Rojas, a Latina pre-K teacher at Cole, said of the parents, "They are just busy. They don't have enough time to spend with their children and talk to them when they're little.... Sometimes parents have to work so much."

A teacher-directed style of communication with parents described the overall nature of teachers' strategies in dealing with this issue in order to improve instruction. Ms. Rodgers, a white pre-K teacher, said the parents' role in children's education was crucial. "We're a team," she said. "It's truly a triangle that we're all working together." Despite the team language, teachers' efforts to involve parents generally emphasized getting parents to follow directions. This type of communication was typified by Ms. Villareal as she described her interactions with Spanish-speaking parents:

> I do tell the parents, "You're responsible for getting your child to do one sheet at night." I'll call the parents and say, "Well, you know his homework folder wasn't in his backpack," and most of the time the parent will bring it, like, at that very minute because they say, "Oh, yeah I forgot to," because I do tell them, "You are the adult. You need to be responsible for putting and checking your child's backpack together before he leaves." But ultimately I do kind of put it on the parents.

Thus, teachers indicated that they could not do their jobs without support from parents, and many said, fairly or unfairly, that they were not getting that help. They said they would be better able to meet the routine challenges of early education and the extra challenges of English language learners if they could more consistently partner with parents.

Returning to the Classroom Data

The interviews with teachers (the talking) suggested three general reasons for the disparity between primarily Spanish and English classrooms in instruction in the development of core skills for academic learning that was observed in the CLASS data (the watching). One of these perceived reasons, literacy challenges, tied into two of the a priori risk mechanisms from figure 5.1, time constraints and perceived instructional fit. Teachers said teaching English language learners was harder than teaching other children in part because of juggling language instruction with their own more substantively focused academic goals. The two other major themes (socioeconomic challenges and parent-related challenges) tied into one of the a priori mechanisms from figure 5.1, perceived instructional fit, and represented emergent themes. Teachers said teaching English language learners was harder than teaching other children in part because what was happening in families and communities affected the teachers' expectations of the children as well as how much they felt equipped to serve them.

One a priori mechanism from figure 5.1, however, was something that we rarely if ever heard from teachers in our discussions with them. That risk factor, compensation, suggested that teachers who perceived major challenges to improving the basic and higher-order skills of English language learners might downplay the development of more concretely academic components of school readiness and concentrate instead on developing more socioemotional components of school readiness. Perhaps because of the negative connotations of compensation, no teachers really engaged with this topic, but the CLASS data revealed some evidence for it. In short, consistent disparities between primarily Spanish-speaking classrooms and other classrooms in instructional support (the CLASS dimension tapping conceptual instruction) did not extend to the CLASS dimensions (emotional support, classroom organization) tapping socioemotional and behavioral aspects of the classroom (table 5.2).

In pre-K in SWISD, primarily Spanish classrooms did lag behind primarily English classrooms in these other instructional processes, but the disparities were smaller and less consistent than the disparity in instructional support. For emotional support, the overall difference between primarily English and Spanish classrooms equaled 9 percent *SD*, but this total score subsumed variation across subscales. Primarily Spanish classrooms looked equal to or better than primarily English classrooms in positive climate and negative climate, which was reverse-coded so that higher scores equal less negative climate, but they lagged behind in respect for students' perspectives and teacher sensitivity. For classroom organization, the primarily Spanish classrooms were generally lower on all subscales, but the largest disparity was for instructional learning formats (39% *SD*). Looking across the emotional support and classroom organization data, the largest disparities between primarily Spanish and English classrooms were for subscales similar in spirit to the instructional support dimension.

In kindergarten, the primarily Spanish classrooms scored lower on emotional support and its subscales. They had no direct advantage for positive climate, as they did in pre-K, and they fared particularly low on respect for students' perspectives (77% *SD*). Interestingly, these primarily Spanish classrooms scored higher than primarily English classrooms on some subscales of classroom organization, such as behavior management (71% *SD*) and productivity (93% *SD*). The one subscale on which they appeared to be

Table 5.2. Mean CLASS scores for dimensions beyond instructional support, by grade level and classroom language instruction

	\multicolumn{5}{c}{Mean (Standard Deviation)}
		\multicolumn{2}{c}{Pre-K}	\multicolumn{2}{c}{Kindergarten}
	All	Spanish	English	Spanish	English
Main domain ratings					
Emotional support	5.15	5.20	5.28	4.62	5.19
	(.91)	(1.04)	(.61)	(.86)	(.70)
Classroom organization	4.99	4.84	5.16	5.23	5.19
	(.82)	(.94)	(.65)	(.60)	(.57)
Emotional support items					
Positive climate	5.01	5.05	4.91	4.87	5.22
	(1.15)	(1.37)	(.92)	(.61)	(.69)
Negative climate	6.11	6.32	5.97	5.53	5.89
	(.99)	(1.01)	(.60)	(1.57)	(.51)
Respect for students' perspectives	4.83	4.77	5.30	4.00	4.89
	(1.09)	(1.16)	(.71)	(1.22)	(.96)
Teacher sensitivity	4.67	4.65	4.94	4.07	4.78
	(1.04)	(1.17)	(.88)	(.72)	(.76)
Classroom organization					
Behavior management	4.76	5.19	5.33	6.27	5.56
	(.99)	(.80)	(.68)	(.64)	(.19)
Productivity	5.37	5.19	5.33	6.30	5.56
	(.79)	(.80)	(.68)	(.64)	(.19)
Instructional learning formats	4.85	4.69	5.30	4.40	5.22
	(1.08)	(1.12)	(.67)	(1.64)	(.69)
n	44	25	11	5	3

at a disadvantage was instructional learning formats (76% *SD*), the subscale most closely related to cognitively stimulating instructional practices.

In sum, less consistent and generally smaller disparities between primarily Spanish classrooms and other classrooms appeared in the emotional support and classroom organization domains than in the instructional support dimensions. Furthermore, within these two other domains, primarily Spanish classrooms were similar to the general pattern of instructional support for the classroom processes most relevant to instruction directly tied to building academic and cognitive skills, as opposed to behavioral management and facilitating socioemotional development.

A Double Disadvantage?

What we saw in SWISD pre-K and kindergarten classrooms suggested that cognitively stimulating instruction might be more difficult for teachers in classrooms serving English language learners than in other kinds of classrooms. What we heard from teachers revealed perceptions about what those difficulties are. A general theme was that focusing on cognitively stimulating instruction in early childhood education classrooms is challenging in and of itself and that this challenge could be intensified by some special circumstances that go along with balancing such instruction with English skill development. The following three circumstances in particular stood out:

- *Double duty.* Many teachers said they did not have enough time in the day to cultivate critical thinking skills in instruction while also addressing the initial language challenges of English language learners.
- *Catch-up.* Some teachers said English language learners came into their classrooms less equipped to engage with the kinds and levels of instruction that they desired to teach, because of a variety of out-of-school obstacles, and they altered their goals and practices in response until they thought such students were ready.
- *Trade-offs.* Some teachers of English language learners appeared to dilute instructional practices directly tied to the development of critical thinking skills in order to focus on more basic skill development or on socioemotional school readiness.

The teachers' perceptions are just that, perceptions. Their remarks reflect what teachers think and feel, but as the classroom observations revealed, teachers' perceptions probably both reflect and drive what they experience on the job. The perceptions undoubtedly were colored by ethnic differences between white teachers and Latina/o families and, among Latina/o teachers and families, by class differences and differences in family immigration histories. There are indeed many divides that separate early childhood education classrooms serving English language learners, and teachers and parents as well as children may not see these divides for what they are. There are other biases at work here too, including the human tendency to be much more critical of others and the larger environment than of oneself.

Still, what we saw and heard in SWISD convinced us that early childhood education classrooms serving young Latina/o English language learners were less cognitively stimulating than classrooms serving other groups of children for reasons both practical and problematic. A main argument I make in this book is that early education classrooms involve many different instructional and interactional processes and should be oriented toward developing school readiness in many diverse ways, not just through the traditional lens of core academic subjects and skills. The development of critical thinking skills to be leveraged in future academic pursuits is one piece of the puzzle. If young English language learners are missing out on this piece at the starting line, some long-term goals of early educational investments in this population could be undercut (Burchinal et al., 2010; Downer et al., 2012; Hamre et al., 2010; Justice et al., 2008). Much of what is going on in these classrooms is positive, but they could be doing more to stimulate cognitive development and prepare students for the academic tasks of elementary school. Consequently, Latina/o English language learners are at a disadvantage not only because of family-school language barriers but also because of what kind of instruction they are exposed to at school. It could be called a "double disadvantage" (Crosnoe, 2005).

CONCLUSION
The Big Picture

Above all else, this book is anchored in the starting line metaphor. If the educational career is a long marathon with major consequences for the future for self and society, we must make sure that all children have a fair shot at competing in the marathon (Lee & Burkham, 2002). One way to do so is to engage in serious efforts to ensure that all children take their places at the starting line of the marathon with the same level of preparation. Increasing equity at the starting line, with no one getting a head start or an unfair advantage or disadvantage, is the basic motivating logic behind the movement to invest in public early childhood education, both nationally and in Texas. That movement has significantly increased access to early childhood education for many groups of children in the United States who otherwise might have missed out on the opportunity. More and more, though, educators, policy makers, and parents are recognizing that access to early childhood education alone is not sufficient to promote equity at the starting line. What happens inside early childhood education classrooms once they are accessed really does. This critical assessment of the starting line metaphor led directly to the driving questions for the research presented in this book: What about early childhood education for Latina/o children is working, and what needs to be improved?

To conclude the book, I look into what can be ascertained by asking the driving questions about the starting line of the educational career, the answers that emerged, and the newer questions that were sparked. To get into all of that, let me first go back to the magic of mayhem that I have seen in early childhood education classrooms over many years. That sensory overload is all about an abundance of often joyous activity, with children in perpetual motion, teachers trying to keep up, and the constant and often very loud noise of teaching and learning. Children in such classrooms engage with numbers, letters, and other lessons with the same gusto that they run around on the playground or eat snacks; they possess an incredible energy. Their teachers do more than wade through or manage; they throw themselves in, matching that energy with a commitment of their own to make their classrooms lively.

Let me be clear, though, that this mayhem is not chaos. The most magical classrooms are like well-oiled machines in which teachers and children are doing their jobs within a broader context of buy-in from administrators, parents, and community members. Something is happening on the ground.

This something that is happening is all part of the amazing experiment playing out on the national level to improve children's lives, enhance the functioning of the educational system, and reduce inequality. That experiment concerns early childhood education serving children from historically disadvantaged and disenfranchised segments of the US population. It represents an ambitious agenda of policy and practice that has been moving forward in fits and starts over several decades, and it is one area in which interdisciplinary scholarship is helping to lead. The exceptionally well done evaluations of Head Start (such as Puma et al., 2010), of many state pre-K programs (Gormley et al., 2005), and of smaller, "boutique" early childhood interventions (Heckman, 2006) have pointed out what is being done right, where things go wrong, and what the stakes are. Those evaluations, in turn, have been informed by smaller-scale studies in various states and local communities that explore what is going on in early childhood programs that represent both the promise and pitfalls of efforts to help children at the starting line.

The research that I, with the help of my students, conducted for this book to address its driving questions is part of that long tradition of incremental gains in policy-relevant knowledge through the accumulation of study upon study. One of my main goals, as it has been throughout my career, has been to shine a light on young Latina/o children from low-income families, particularly immigrant families, within the US educational system. Often, these children are invisible in research and policy but are under a harsh spotlight colored by the anti-immigration rhetoric and policies that have increased in recent years. They need to be in a spotlight of concern and support, as they are making up an ever-larger share of students in an educational system that has historically not served them well. Turning that around and serving them well is necessary not just for ethical reasons but also because of demographic reality.

In focusing on young Latina/o children from low-income families, I felt it important to conduct more in-depth exploration within schools and communities, in part because getting into the weeds can be a good thing for research but also because I value listening to human voices in ways that large-scale evaluations do not easily allow. Texas and SWISD in particular made a good place to do that, and I do not think that merely because I live here. Texas is where that demographic reality facing so much of the country has already been happening for a long time; it offers a microcosm of a larger demographic trend converging with a major educational policy movement that enables exploration in ways that speak to the future.

So, my team and I waded into the magical mayhem of SWISD, listening to voices through hours of interviews with parents and teachers of young children and watching activities and interactions through hours of observations of classrooms from pre-K through second grade. Guided by the underlying questions, we heard and saw so much during this time that I often felt hard pressed to draw out simple and straightforward take-home messages. Even though I struggled through to eventually do so, I know that those messages by no means represent any sort of bottom-line conclusion. Again, my goal was to shine the light, figure out what was happening, and determine whether what was happening spoke to what needed to be maintained, built on, done away with, or corrected moving forward. In that spirit, let me explain what I observed, what lessons I learned from what I observed, how I can apply those lessons to inform policy and practice, and how these lessons and their applications can be extended by future research.

What I Observed

Following the blueprint derived from contextual systems theory that emphasizes the power of connections in early childhood education for Latina/o children from low-income families, we covered 58 pre-K, kindergarten, first grade, and second grade classrooms in nine elementary schools in SWISD over an extended period. That blueprint highlights two contextual connections, in-school connections in an alignment of classrooms within and across grades and out-of-school connections linking parents, teachers, and community members; the blueprint also features two connected processes, cross-philosophy exchanges of academic and developmental approaches to teaching and learning and cross-activity exchanges for building language and academic skills. Whether through watching or listening with an emphasis on connections, here is what we observed.

Horizontal alignment across classrooms was easier and more common than vertical alignment among classrooms. Teachers tended to see their same-grade colleagues as their natural communities within the schools and spend significant time coordinating with them to ensure consistency across classrooms. At the same time, they were less likely to have the same perceptions and behaviors regarding teachers in contiguous grades within the primary grade system. This widespread horizontal alignment was a function of proximity and professional development. Classrooms in the same grade tended to be located next to each other, and teachers in the same grades had more opportunities to interact. And the professional development programs that the pre-K teachers engaged in encouraged their coordination and provided a similar agenda for all. There were no similarly strong forces encouraging vertical alignment, and those interactions and relations either did not really ever form or withered once they formed. There was also a tendency for pre-K to be seen as separate from the rest of elementary school, implicitly or even explicitly segregating pre-K teachers from the rest of the school personnel.

Not surprisingly, then, horizontal alignment was particularly strong and the discrepancy between horizontal and vertical alignment was particularly great at the Cole Pre-K Campus. This campus brought together many different pre-K teachers in the same building, separate from other primary grades and under an explicit mission of fostering a positive pre-K experience. Cole brought pre-K teachers together but increased their separation from other teachers. When vertical alignment did arise, it seemed to be fostered by an element of school structure in the smaller school sizes and fewer classrooms per grade and an aspect of teacher background, that of teachers' experiences in multiple grades over the course of a career, allowing a cross-grade perspective that could be construed as a form of self-alignment. The data also suggested that both horizontal and vertical alignment but especially the latter arose out of a positive school climate overall that encouraged a sense of community and teamwork among teachers at the school level. Based on what many teachers told us and what we saw on our own, that climate was more likely a cause rather than an effect of widespread alignment. Thus, alignment is likely to fluctuate as a function of teachers' own motivations, the organizational structures of schools that shaped interactions and goals, and the support and encouragement of school administration.

The talk about family-school-community partnerships did not always match the reality. Teachers and parents in SWISD highly valued the idea of building partnerships between home and school and to a lesser extent the larger community in which they were situated. Yet these partnerships that they were proud of, the teams they formed, tended to be unequal, unidirectional, and shallow. They were controlled by teachers within a narrow scope that did not provide much agency for parents and made them vulnerable to having their values about education and parenting misinterpreted, as with the values of *respeto* and *bien educado*. In short, teachers told parents what to do at home and how to support their children in school. There was far less opportunity for or even awareness of the need for the opportunity for parents to have input into what was going on in school, to share insights about children with school personnel, to engage in their own forms of learning activities with children outside of school that could be respected by school personnel, or to voice and enact their values.

One example of this imbalance within cross-context partnerships that was clear to us exposed socioeconomic and ethnic divides between home and school. Many teachers recognized that a family's low socioeconomic status or membership in a historically disadvantaged ethnic group could influence how parents approached schools and the resources they could marshal to support their children's education. Their interpretation of these socioeconomic and ethnic influences, however, was highly internal rather than external. Teachers' perceptions of such families tended to cast them as uninvolved in schooling because of something about the parents themselves, that they did not care, could not be bothered, were too passive, or did not know what they were doing. The teachers' interpretations did not tend to touch on such barriers as the practical constraints of poverty, language divides, and discrimination that could keep even the most motivated and invested parents from participating in visible school-based activities. Tellingly, teachers who were Latina/o themselves were more likely to wade into the external barriers than white or African American teachers. Informed by their familiarity with parents' values, they provided a more well-rounded discussion of why their students' parents did or did not interact with them or engage in teamwork behaviors.

Thus, as in so many other schools and districts, efforts to build family-school-community partnerships as a means of reducing educational inequalities in SWISD could have the potential to exacerbate those inequalities. That could happen if enriching the substance of these partnerships is not given as much as attention as increasing the frequency.

Different kinds of positive learning and teaching processes tend to go together within classrooms, leading to stark differences across classrooms. CLASS has three main dimensions: emotional support, tapping into the socioemotional warmth and supportiveness of teacher-student interactions; classroom organization, the ways teachers oversee classroom activities and keep children on task; and instructional support, the degree to which teachers engage in classroom activities and interactions that are most likely to encourage deep thinking and the development of higher-order analytical skills. Overall, the SWISD classrooms scored higher than or at least on par with national averages, but they tended to do so or not do so in a consistent manner. Classrooms that scored relatively high on one tended to score relatively high on the others, and classrooms that scored relatively low on one tended to score relatively low on the others. The goal was classrooms that were socioemotionally and academically supportive, and there is certainly more to do to reach that goal.

The classrooms we classified as being socioemotionally supportive and having academic scaffolding really did not meet the bar because their instructional support score, the linchpin of academic scaffolding, tended to be in the low moderate to low range rather than high or even moderately high. This classification was warranted in the sense that such classrooms were above the national average on instructional support, but that leaves much room for improvement on that score. The most notable trend in this investigation was that instructional support was always lower than the other CLASS dimensions no matter the classroom. No classroom was high or even moderate in instructional support without also scoring high in the other, more socioemotional or managerial dimensions of classroom processes. Stimulating cognitive development and academic learning, therefore, consistently seemed to be the weak link. In particular, the Cole Pre-K Campus tended to be very good at the socioemotional supportiveness but to have more trouble linking that to academic scaffolding. Teachers in classrooms conducted primarily in Spanish tended to be on the extremes, overrepresented on the "All good things go together" front and on the "No good things go together" front. Teachers in other kinds of classrooms hewed more to the middle ground and avoided the extremes.

As so defined, the key to SWISD classrooms that were socioemotionally supportive and had academic scaffolding seemed to be the coupling of teachers who were responsive to and respectful of their students but also engaged in language modeling with children. They tended to be quite responsive to children's needs while also encouraging cognitive development through complex language with children. They cared about and supported the children and pressed and challenged them. Teachers who could pull off this seemingly important duality appeared to operate within the false divide between developmentally appropriate practices and the standards movement while addressing the limitations of and building on the strengths of both. They viewed the development of social and emotional skills as intertwined with the development of cognitive and academic skills rather than as mutually exclusive. Still, their bottom-line priority was the latter, with the former as a means to an end. This spirit seemed to be pronounced when they faced children with special academic needs such as English language learners.

Thus, constructing socioemotionally supportive classrooms appeared to be easier than constructing academic scaffolding in classrooms, but teachers who were better than most on the scaffolding part were consistently good on the support part and viewed the two as synergistic rather than competing.

Cognitively stimulating instruction is difficult in the face of other instructional challenges. Primarily Spanish classrooms encompass different English language supports for children developing English skills but not dual-language programs, which aim to cultivate bilingualism more generally. The primarily Spanish classes in our study were more likely than other classrooms to be either high or low in coupling academic scaffolding with socioemotional supportiveness. On the downside, such classrooms were more likely to be at the low end of the distribution of the indicators of academic scaffolding; that is, they were low on the subdimensions of instructional support while also being low on any subdimensions of emotional support and classroom organization that were closely related to instructional support. Further analysis revealed that primarily Spanish classrooms tended to be relatively low in activities and interactions most closely linked to the development of higher-order analytical skills such as interpretation and complex language, especially in pre-K.

Interviews with teachers revealed that they felt like they were struggling to meet the language needs of English language learners in their classrooms while also pursuing the broader academic goals of pre-K. When they talked about such struggles, though, they tended to conflate children's general literacy (understanding and using oral and written language) with children's English literacy (understanding and using English, including written English). They also focused a great deal on perceived deficits related to low socioeconomic status, hinting and sometimes outright saying that children from lower-status families might not be up to the challenge and that the parents were not investing in helping the children succeed. The teachers perceived family socioeconomic statuses as difficulties imposed upon them, and they tried to find ways to solve those difficulties or make up for them. Notably, no teacher who engaged in conversation with us was aligned with our concept of compensation, that is, focusing on building other kinds of skills with English language learners even as the stimulation of cognitive and academic skills faded. Yet, the CLASS analysis indicated that primarily Spanish classrooms had bigger divides between socioemotionally supportive instruction and academic scaffolding. Students in those classrooms seemed to be getting something but losing something.

Teachers in primarily Spanish classrooms often felt they were doing double duty relative to other teachers because they needed to simultaneously help children develop English proficiency and engage in the usual academic activities of pre-K classrooms with English speakers. Some reacted to this double duty in ways that promoted the overall learning of children, while others reacted by emphasizing the classroom processes less directly and explicitly linked to higher-order skill-building.

What I Learned

Having summarized what we observed for each of the four main parts of the blueprint grounded in the driving questions that guided this study, I want to share the lessons I have learned from all of this observation in SWISD. Sometimes, I admit, I learned them slowly. These lessons cut across the four parts of the blueprint, weaving together the watching and listening we did to gain a sense of the bigger picture.

Communication is a key element of contextual connections that has to be purposefully cultivated. At face value, family-school partnerships existed across all schools in SWISD that we studied, and consistently there was spoken support for building and maintaining these partnerships. Clearly, parents, school personnel, and community members were speaking with each other and generally interacting, but that communication masked something that was often shallower than the term "communication" implies. It was talk but not conversation. Similarly, alignment was by no means a foreign concept to SWISD teachers in most schools, and it was a concept that held value across schools. Yet, especially with vertical alignment, talk about alignment was not often matched with real action toward alignment. In partnerships and alignment, lines of communication seemed to be open to connect disparate actors in the early childhood education of young Latina/o children from low-income families. The lines of communication proved to be necessary but not sufficient conditions for living up to the promise of big ideas for interactional change like partnership or alignment.

Real partnerships and alignments need something deeper, something more mutual and sustained over longer periods of time. They require true relationships. With family-school-community partnerships, a variety of factors are keeping communication from becoming conversation. Teachers talk to parents without receiving much talk from parents, or they do a lot of talking past one another, because there is a clear imbalance between the two sides. The teachers are professionals, often white, in charge of the children's educational fortunes in school; they often are viewed by low-income Latina/o parents as authority figures, and the parents tend to respect that. The teachers may not realize their power, but they have it, and it can silence parents from expressing what they want for their children and blind the teachers to what parents do for their children. Parents on the other side of this imbalance may think that their role is to listen and receive, and they may be reluctant to offer their thoughts or ask their questions. On the teacher side, there is often inertia as they go about what they routinely do without eliciting feedback unless it is immediately forthcoming. They may also carry with them assumptions, colored by race/ethnicity and socioeconomic status in ways often hard to see, that parents will not have concrete input into the educational process, that parents need to be guided just as their children are, and that values of *respeto* and the like are not inherently academic. So, teachers and parents follow standard practices and interact in prescribed and often required school-based meetings that fall back into the model of the school figure telling the home or community figure what is going on in school without recognizing that this information sharing is not an exchange.

The same is true for alignment. Horizontal alignment is just easier in many ways than vertical alignment, so teachers may fall into predictable patterns of interaction and communication that represent a form of stasis. Schools are organized by grade, and that kind of organizational proximity matters in fostering relationships within grades but without the same kind of support for cross-grade relationships. That relationship-building and maintenance then creates a comfort level that is self-sustaining. The overlay of professional development programs focusing on within-grade processes strengthens these tendencies. Over time, horizontal alignment can just happen without as much intentional strategy, while vertical alignment still requires intent and dedicated effort. Teachers may value both horizontal and vertical alignment, but the former can come more naturally than the latter and provide more opportunity for communication to deepen and broaden into conversation. It just happens.

Activities that underlie the development of cognitive and academic skills are the most vulnerable elements of connected processes. Facilitating the development of what are often referred to as higher-order skills, such as interpretation, analysis, and complex language, also presents a higher order of difficulty for teachers. Children may not respond well to prompts or consistently engage in question-and-answer feedback loops. Their language may be slow to develop, and they will not always get it when teachers lead them into something more challenging. These kinds of activities might not appear to bring clear returns, at least in the short term. When teachers engage in socioemotionally supportive activities or use more managerial or organizational behaviors, they are likely to see the results. Those results may come in the form of students seeming happier and behaving better, classrooms that are calmer and run more smoothly, and easier flow in the classroom day. Those kinds of visible returns then encourage more attention to that dimension of teaching or classroom management.

That teacher activities geared toward cognitive skill development appeared to be less common in classrooms that predominantly served English language learners is perhaps telling. On the practical side, there is only so much time in the classroom day, and efforts to help children learn English—an immediate concern—may crowd out efforts to help them build more general cognitive or academic skills. In a more complicated way, there could also be a tendency toward compensation that goes beyond the possibility of a zero-sum game in time. That compensation would entail unconscious or even conscious shifts in attention toward instructional activities that teachers perceive as easier and more likely to achieve a desired result such as socioemotional development or positive behavior. In SWISD classrooms we saw some evidence of both. Although both could be considered problems in terms of what English language learners might be losing in the classroom, I am also sympathetic toward teachers who may feel overwhelmed. They need more support to overcome the challenges they face that other early childhood education teachers do not.

Of note is that some evidence suggested that classrooms predominantly serving English language learners were not uniformly low in academic scaffolding. These classrooms were more likely than other classrooms to couple socioemotional supportiveness and academic scaffolding or to have neither. Teachers in primarily Spanish classrooms populated both ends of the spectrum, and the average of the two gave a more pessimistic picture of instructional quality in these classrooms than looking at the full distribution of classrooms serving English language learners, which included bright spots and worrisome spots. Guidance for how to raise the overall level of academic scaffolding in classrooms with English language speakers may be found by looking deeper into the bright spots. Some teachers seemed to have a psychological benefit akin to a growth mindset (Dweck, 2008). When challenged, they doubled down and worked harder to find solutions. Still, the motivations for teachers providing both support and scaffolding cannot solely be psychological. Schools are formal organizations staffed by professionals; problems in schools and remedies for those problems also come from the ways teachers engage in professional activities within contexts that make doing their jobs easier or harder.

Common ground is essential to contextual connections and connected processes and requires attention to potential fissures. Parents, school personnel, and community members need to feel like they are on the same team. A shared purpose can go a long way toward building and supporting family-school-community partnerships and facilitating the depth and breadth of communication as a foundation for those partnerships. Something similar applies to alignment within schools. Some teachers have more common ground than others by virtue of their equivalent positions at school or proximity to each other, and the ease that goes along with that common ground can encourage the effort needed to make alignment a reality.

For family-school-community partnerships, I learned that shared ethnicity helps to provide common ground. Latina/o parents felt more comfortable with Latina/o teachers than they did with white teachers or African American teachers. In part that was because Latina/o teachers and other Latina/o school personnel were more likely to speak Spanish, which broke down the obvious impediment of the language barrier. And the apparent value of ethnic matching went beyond language. It was about a feeling, real or perceived, right or wrong, of mutual understanding. Parents trusted Latina/o teachers more, and our time interviewing teachers in SWISD suggested that this trust was not misguided. Latina/o teachers consistently were more likely to give Latina/o parents the benefit of the doubt. Furthermore, they generally had more nuanced and realistic views of Latina/o parents' engagement in their children's educational careers, perhaps influenced by the same Latina/o socialization values such as *bien educado*. They looked deeper into the families' lives and circumstances in ways that other teachers seemed to have trouble doing. Within this common ground, though, there remained the fissure of socioeconomic disparities. Even when parents and teachers were Latina/o, the parents usually approached the relationship from a socioeconomically disadvantaged position, particularly in educational attainment and experience in the US educational system. Even sympathetic teachers often lost sight of this difference and seemed unaware that it meant parents and teachers had different vantage points on children's education, and that difference contributed to a power imbalance.

For alignment, being in the same grade level clearly provided the common ground that supported alignment. Teachers in the same grade level saw each other as natural teammates, and communication flowed in a way that allowed it to deepen into true conversation. They saw each other a lot and were often required to meet and plan curricula and schedules. They also had a sense of shared purpose that was defined by their grade-level goals. Horizontal alignment was not a far reach and required little purposeful action or dedicated effort. Vertical alignment, however, required motivation, planning, and follow-through. Teachers in different grade levels did not see each other as enemies or strangers by any means, but they tended to stand at a remove from each other. Communication was infrequent or sporadic enough or untethered to curricular missions and goals that it did not naturally flow toward deepening and broadening into conversation. At the same time, pre-K teachers appeared to be isolated from other teachers, lending credence to the opinions of some that elementary school teachers may not see pre-K as real school. For these reasons, vertical alignment, which is crucial to creating an early education system supporting children's cumulative progression of learning, may require a more top-down approach. That approach could include external incentives for bringing teachers together regularly across grade levels and seeing each other as a team.

There is common ground among school personnel and between school personnel and those they serve, and that common ground can be used to build a foundation. However, building such a foundation is facilitated by also identifying and understanding the weak spots in that common ground.

Organizational structures can promote or undermine contextual connections and connected processes in concrete ways. Continuing with the discussion of alignment, one clear factor in differentiating horizontal and vertical alignment supports the horizontal and interferes with the vertical; that is the location of pre-K classrooms on a pre-K campus or within the home elementary school. This pattern speaks to the concrete effects of organizational arrangements on in-class and cross-class processes. In short, organization matters.

The Cole Pre-K Campus created a closed universe of pre-K teachers that allowed, encouraged, and strengthened communication among them. Furthermore, it connected pre-K teachers across elementary schools, considering that different schools placed their pre-K programs at Cole. In this way, Cole succeeded not just at horizontal alignment across teachers in a grade but also at horizontal alignment across teachers in a grade across the district. It appeared to do so at a cost, though, as it simultaneously separated pre-K teachers and classrooms from other teachers and classrooms in the educational system.

Whether the gains of horizontal alignment outweighed the costs to vertical alignment remains an open question with practical consequences, and this question needs to be addressed. After all, vertical alignment is generally low, and not just in SWISD (Kauerz, 2006; Pelletier & Corter, 2006). Thus, organizational barriers to vertical alignment might not make a meaningful difference beyond what is already constraining it or interfering with it. There is a common tendency for pre-K to be seen as "other" in elementary schools. That real or perceived isolation of pre-K teachers and classrooms, which, again, is not specific to SWISD at all (Bogard & Takanishi, 2005), is another possible reason to consider the balance between the gains and costs of the Cole pre-K structure. Physically housing pre-K classrooms in elementary schools could break down one organizational barrier to vertical alignment but might have little impact if more social-psychological barriers still exist.

There are no easy fixes to such challenges, but these kinds of tensions within the teaching staffs of schools require special attention moving forward. They concern the value of situating early childhood education within a concrete physical space and not just in the more abstract realm of educational policy or theory.

Applying the Lessons

Increasingly, I have aligned myself with the field of translational social science, meaning conducting research with the explicit purpose of drawing out and communicating lessons for policy and practice. There are different levels and degrees of translation, from basic research relevant to policy goals all the way up to explicit two-way policy-evaluating and research-inspiring partnerships between scholars and practitioners. My study in SWISD falls more in the middle of the spectrum. It entailed conventional community-based data collection focusing on Latina/o children from low-income families. The study was designed also after discussions with school personnel and with funders from a private foundation aiming to support policy reforms to promote early childhood education in this large and growing population. Reflecting the translational foundation for this study, therefore, I did not stop with lessons learned but tried to link those lessons to specific discussions and debates about policy intervention and school reform.

Use mediators to deepen school-based discussions and conversations. Schools are good meeting points for activities that can connect them with families and communities, as they have an administrative apparatus for organizing events and space to hold them. Yet, the shallow communication versus deep conversation divide that appeared in our analysis of family-school-community partnerships in SWISD suggests that they require more tending than letting them organically grow. If the obstacle to partnerships in low-income Latina/o communities is not only a lack of talking but talking past each other or talking from different starting assumptions, then the talk needs to be led, managed, and curated by people who can identify the talking past each other and see other starting assumptions such as family liaisons or advocacy groups. A community-based mediator who understands the families being served by the school and has some tie to the school, perhaps a parent of a former student, may be able to work with school personnel to foster more enriched discussions that then lead to deeper communication. These mediators would be in a good position to translate school talk to parents not simply in the literal sense of English to Spanish but also in the figurative sense of making unwritten rules of the educational system clearer. They could also help parents share their insights and values with teachers. A shared understanding of what children need is the objective, but I am not convinced it can be attained without a little help.

To this point I have not written much about the parent-support specialist at Cole Pre-K Campus. As a bilingual Latina who lived in the area and whose children had attended Cole-linked schools, she proved to be an amazing support for parents and someone teachers also trusted. Not only did she literally speak the same Spanish language as the parents, she figuratively shared a language with them in the form of values and ideas about Latina/o socialization of children. She would be an ideal mediator; other parent support specialists I saw, not so much. Thus, a natural position for this kind of role is already in place in many schools serving low-income Latina/o communities, but helping the person in that position take on that role requires dedicated support.

The same thinking goes for alignment. Even removing barriers that obstruct interaction and discussion among teachers within or across grades cannot ensure that communication will deepen and broaden into conversation. A mediator, perhaps a teacher or administrator with deep experience in a grade or across grades, needs to help get the conversation going, identify roadblocks, and point out the unspoken that needs to be spoken. Just as with family-school-partnerships, a mediator should not be someone with no stake in them or working from a place of neutrality. The mediator should have a stake in all sides working from a place of full investment. If children from low-income Latina/o families do benefit more from investments in their educational journeys such as alignment and family-school-community partnerships, that benefit adds motivation to take the relatively easy step of getting such mediators in place.

Emphasize the value of interactional supports for critical thinking in professional development. The perceived trade-offs of instructional activities that support positive socioemotional development and those that support academic and cognitive development can trigger tired discussions about soft versus hard skills. The "versus" part misses the point. Soft-skill development supports hard-skill development, and attending to development in its many domains is ultimately a good way to help young children.

What does that multifaceted support, attending to development in its many domains, mean from a practical standpoint? If the academic, cognitive side of things is more vulnerable to the many demands on early childhood education classrooms than other classroom processes, as it is in SWISD and on the national level, then that side should be more explicitly fostered within the overall context of constructing a positive classroom environment for children. Professional development programs need to provide more direct and concrete guidance to help teachers integrate such activities into their daily plans and to attend to how much they are actually doing. Ideally, that kind of guidance could target the daily challenges that could interfere with teachers' abilities to follow through consistently on their motivations to provide instructional support to young children. There are programs to foster the management and leadership of multicultural classrooms, but they need not be limited to the conceptual components of that mission, such as fostering empathy and facilitating equal participation. Practical components of that mission also need to be addressed, such as managing class time, in what can seem like a zero-sum game.

Put extra weight into diversifying teaching staffs. The changing demographic make-up of the teaching staff of US schools has not kept up with the changing demographic composition among students. Given the degree to which common ground can foster deeper and broader conversations among the stakeholders of early childhood education, the frequent mismatch of school staffs and the communities they serve could pose problems.

Diversity issues are recognized by school personnel and communities as well as by policy makers trying to support both. The disparity is a pipeline problem, and there is no clear way to solve it in the short term. Incentivizing partnerships between school districts and university-based schools of educational training is one possible path, as is reducing obstacles to teachers entering the profession in nontraditional ways such as mid-career professionals in other fields switching to teaching, Diversity cannot be approached too narrowly. Yes, racial/ethnic diversity matters in a diverse and segregated educational system, but it is not the only dimension of diversity that matters. Linguistic barriers and socioeconomic stratification are dimensions of diversity and inequality that go beyond race/ethnicity even within racially/ethnically homogeneous schools and communities.

Given my focus in this book, the needs of the state in which I reside, and a future in which Latina/o children make up an ever-larger share of the American student population, I am going to emphasize the value of explicitly targeting a specific segment of the population for recruitment into teaching careers. That segment includes the large number of Latina/o youth who are or will be first-generation college students. They will bring a range of perspectives to teaching that cross many divides and create common ground in the context of a new demographic reality.

Encourage fluidity among grade levels and positions. The concept of "self-alignment" really struck me during our time in SWISD. This term refers to the ways teachers who have gained experience teaching in multiple grades can accrue some of the benefits of vertical alignment even when vertical alignment is not actually happening. They understand where their students are coming from and then where they are going next, and they plan curricular activities and goals accordingly.

In some ways, the self-alignment concept goes against the idea that teachers should gain deep experience within their grades. They should. I just want to suggest that deep experience within a grade may not align well with the recognition of early childhood education as part of a larger system. Alignment is an approach that does promote that recognition, but vertical alignment is hard to get going. Self-alignment offers a possible motor to get it going. Having teachers rotate through contiguous grades, even if for a short time, could provide them the opportunity to gain more complex perspectives that make vertical alignment easier or even substitute for the lack of it. If so, that rotation would not be something teachers do alone, as it could have benefits for school administrators and parent-support specialists. Their gain in perspectives could also address the tendency for pre-K teachers to be isolated and early childhood education to be viewed as somehow different from elementary school.

Self-alignment is specifically about teachers and managing instruction, but the basic idea that switching roles allows people to understand how all roles come together also applies to family-school-community partnerships. The rotation idea is harder to translate into concrete action for family-school-community partnerships than it is for alignment, but baby steps can produce progress in this area, such as parents shadowing teachers and teachers enrolling their own children in the schools where they teach.

Extended Research

I am trained as a basic rather than applied researcher of quantitative population rather than community-based studies of children, families, and schools. As such, I approached this study mixing classroom observations with qualitative interviews in a sample of classrooms in a single district as a departure in many ways. I have done qualitative research within schools and districts (Crosnoe, 2011; Crosnoe et al., 2015), but I have also linked that qualitative research to national-level research to combine the big picture of inequality with detailed insights of everyday life at the same time. My goal here has been to shine a light in a preliminary way. What I mean by that is that I want to use the insights gleaned from my time in SWISD to point to where the discussion about the early childhood education of Latina/o children from low-income families might go next and then to actually go there in future translational research. For me, that means using the research featured here and the dialogues it starts with schools and other stakeholders in early childhood education to build a new line of research that emphasizes generalizability and establishes cause and effect. To that end, I lay out what I see as the pieces of this study that need to be further developed and extended to get the most out of this kind of research.

Flesh out the conceptual blueprint to more fully reflect contextual systems. The blueprint for this study drew on contextual systems theory to emphasize two kinds of classroom connections in the early childhood education of Latina/o children, two external to the classroom and two within classrooms. The theory is much broader than those four connections, so the next steps are to build on that blueprint by both extending out and by digging down.

For example, the community is the broader context in which families and schools are situated, but my foray into communities here mostly concerned community members in general as part of family-school-community partnerships. That is insufficient. One way to get a better handle on community connections to early childhood education is to consider the social networks of Latina/o families with young children in the community. Those social networks are likely to be powerful sources of norms and information about early childhood education, particularly for Latina/o immigrant parents who have not had as much experience with the US educational system as other parents of children in the school. A second way is to consider the civic infrastructure of Latina/o communities (Gamoran et al., 2012; Ressler, 2020). That infrastructure encompasses the array of service providers, nonprofits, businesses, and other organizations and institutions in a community that can connect families and support schools.

As another example, contextual systems theory places the child in the center of the web of interacting processes and contexts around them. For a variety of reasons, I chose not to focus on children in this study beyond observing them in classrooms and interviewing their teachers and parents about them. Instead, I treated the classroom as the unit of analysis to map out the landscape of early childhood education in SWISD. Children's behavior and learning now needs to be better incorporated, including understanding how different Latina/o children may have divergent experiences in the same classrooms. In my past research I have paid special attention to the phenomenon of child elicitation, the ways children's traits, characteristics, or behaviors or others' perceptions of them evoke responses from parents, teachers, and other adults that then shape their development (Ansari & Crosnoe, 2015a, 2015b). The classroom processes I saw in SWISD are not solely dictated by teachers but arise out of teacher-student interactions, so surely children have a role in eliciting those processes that needs to be examined more closely. Latina/o children, after all, are not just recipients of early childhood education. They are drivers too.

Move from exploration to hypothesis-testing. Contextual systems theory oriented me as I entered into my time at SWISD. Following a grounded theory approach, I wanted to look for certain themes and patterns, but I also had to be open to anything new or unexpected I might see. That is the value of exploratory research, observing and learning. Now that I have learned a great deal about on-the-ground action in the early childhood education of Latina/o children from low-income families, I think I am prepared for the next level. Moving to that level involves designing research that takes the answers to my exploratory questions, uses them to craft hypotheses about the predictors and effects of early childhood education in this population, and then tests those hypotheses. I want to take this smaller-scale and primarily qualitative analysis with its own strengths as the basis for a larger-scale and primarily quantitative analysis with different strengths.

Testing hypotheses derived from the conceptual blueprint of this study would involve an expansion of scope. I would need to collect CLASS observation data, survey data from key actors including teachers and parents, contextual data about communities and schools, and administrative data with assessments of and tests from children; the sample would come not just from schools in one district but from districts in Texas. That way, I could estimate associations between key variables, such as parent-teacher ethnic matching as an influence on parent-teacher communication quality, teacher instructional support as an influence on child reading achievement, and classroom language instructional type as an influence on teacher use of cognitive stimulation. Doing so across a much larger and diverse sample would allow me to assess the degree to which those assessments are generalizable, whether they capture the state of the state, so to speak.

These statistical associations, though, will be just that—associations. They will suggest potential patterns of cause and effect but not establish them. Yes, pre-K teachers who engage in more activities to help children develop higher-order thinking skills may have students who do better on achievement tests in kindergarten, but whether one led to the other is not known. Perhaps children who have great learning potential elicit more of that kind of investment from teachers as a form of reverse causality. Perhaps schools with more community resources encourage teachers to engage in more of this activity and promote student achievement simultaneously as a spurious or confounding factor. There is no way to solve such problems without employing an experimental design, but steps can be taken in a nonexperimental data collection to reduce these problems and provide more confidence in the conclusions. These steps mostly involve collecting data longitudinally and drawing on advanced statistics to analyze the longitudinal data; my past and current large-scale data collections in child care centers, elementary schools, and high schools provides a template for doing so.

At some point, the larger-scale study I am building on this preliminary exploratory study will need to be built on even more. Moving beyond the state of Texas to determine the degree to which this state is an outlier, bellwether, or the norm is one way, and eventually adopting an experimental approach to hypothesis-testing is another. That is the way that good translational research proceeds, incrementally, building step by step, even if it takes time.

Better capture the diversity of the young Latina/o experience. Going larger with this line of research is not just about gaining more numbers to improve statistical power. It is about coverage. The more districts and communities in the sample, the more the study can cover the extreme heterogeneity among Latina/o Americans in Texas and in this country. The present study focused on low-income Latina/o families living in a large urban area. Although Latina/o families have a higher rate of poverty than the general population, most are not low-income, yet their children still face obstacles in early childhood education. Similarly, large numbers of Latina/o families residing in suburban and rural areas have children who are entering into different kinds of educational contexts with a wider or narrower array of educational opportunities.

I have explained how four key factors come together within the Latina/o population to increase the need for early childhood education to better serve this population. Those factors are socioeconomic disadvantage, which can reduce access to educational resources; Latina/o ethnicity, which can evoke discrimination and differential treatment; lack of experience with English, which can complicate academic instruction; and cultural barriers, which can lead to misinterpretation and misunderstanding of goals and values. Just because these factors converge statistically among Latina/o Americans does not mean that they converge in all Latina/o families. Sampling is needed for studies of the early childhood education of Latina/o children with attention to heterogeneity within factors; the sample could include families across the socioeconomic spectrum or the language continuum with monolingual English or Spanish at the ends and bilingualism in the middle. The study could explore different combinations of the various dimensions across factors to consider, such as ways the role of bilingualism or cultural values might vary by family socioeconomic status.

As a population scientist who prioritizes generalizable results, I am often guilty of discussing Latina/o children and their families as a single, uniform entity. Exploring variability within generalizable patterns is the way to guard against that shortcoming and more fully capture the Latina/o experience today.

Engage in participatory research rather than scientist-driven scholarship. When I began this study I talked with many stakeholders in early childhood education, from district leaders and personnel to educational scholars to officers in a foundation that funds policy research on Latina/o children. I had a sense of not just what people knew but what they did not know but wanted to know. That sense proved to be quite helpful to me. It helped me focus on some important issues but also held in check some of my preconceived notions. This experience is in line with the growing philosophy of participatory research, which contends that research quality is improved when the subjects of research are involved in conceptualizing the study and advising the researchers on its design from the beginning (Belone et al., 2016; Kemmis & McTaggart, 2005). This approach means that research is not just about a group of people but involves them. It is a bidirectional exchange between the university and the community (Wallerstein & Duran, 2010).

Here is where, despite engaging many stakeholders, my study was not really participatory research: it did not involve Latina/o families and community members from the get-go. The exploratory design of the study was influenced by what educational stakeholders emphasized but not by what was happening with the other community stakeholders in the educational system. Moving forward, any research building on what I have done here needs to start with a community advisory group that connects school personnel with families and community members. That group then would become a mechanism through which a fuller range of perspectives could be reflected in the design of the study as well as in the interpretation of results.

The way research on education, health, crime, and other important issues is conducted in this country is changing as we recraft how we think about translation, who research is for, and what scientific bias might influence the results. That kind of change is especially important when scholars, often white and socioeconomically advantaged ones like me, study groups or communities that have historically been pushed to the margins of society.

Going Forward

Throughout the research that my students (especially Aida and Claude) and I conducted for this book, I observed a great deal and learned far more. Those lessons learned are valuable not just for the scholars studying the early childhood education of young Latina/o children from low-income families now or in the future but also for what federal, state, and local governments can do to support the best interests of such children today and tomorrow. The more who join this cause, the greater the progress that can be achieved.

I opened this book by expressing the sentiment that despite much progress, there is still so much to learn. There is so much to do, too. To repeat myself, we must keep pushing—on both counts.

Works Cited

Adair, J. K. (2014). Agency and expanding capabilities: What it could mean for young children in the early grades. *Harvard Education Review, 84*, 217–241.
Adair, J., & Tobin, J. (2008). Listening to the voices of immigrant parents. In Genishi, C., & Goodwin, A. L. (Eds.), *Diversities in early childhood education: Rethinking and doing* (pp. 137–150). New York, NY: Taylor & Francis.
Alexander, K. L., Entwisle, D. R., & Olson, L. S. (2014). *The long shadow: Family background, disadvantaged urban youth, and the transition to adulthood*. New York, NY: Russell Sage Foundation.
Anderson, S., & Phillips, D. (2017). Is pre-K classroom quality associated with kindergarten and middle-school academic skills? *Developmental Psychology, 53*, 1063–1078.
Andrews, R., Jargowsky, P., & Kuhne, K. (2012). The effects of Texas's targeted prekindergarten program on academic performance. National Bureau of Economic Research Working Paper No. 18598.
Ansari, A., & Crosnoe, R. (2015a). Children's elicitation of changes in parenting during the early childhood years. *Early Childhood Research Quarterly, 32*, 139–149.
Ansari, A., & Crosnoe, R. (2015b). Immigration and the interplay of parenting, preschool enrollment, and young children's academic skills. *Journal of Family Psychology, 29*, 382–393.
Arias, M. B., & Morillo-Campbell, M. (2008). *Promoting ELL parental involvement: Challenges in contested times*. Tempe, AZ: College of Education, Arizona State University.
Arzubiaga, A. E., & Adair, J. (2009). Misrepresentations of language and culture, language and culture as proxies for marginalization. In Murillo, E., Villenas, S., Galván, R., Muñoz, J. S., & Martínez, C., Machado-Casas, M. (Eds.), *The handbook of Latinos and education: Theory, research, and practice* (pp. 301–308). New York, NY: Routledge.
Bailey, D., Duncan, G. J., Odgers, C. L., & Yu, W. (2017). Persistence and fadeout in the impacts of child and adolescent interventions. *Journal of Research on Educational Effectiveness, 10*, 7–39.
Barnett, W. S., & Masse, L. N. (2007). Comparative benefit–cost analysis of the Abe-

cedarian program and its policy implications. *Economics of Education Review, 26,* 113–125.

Bassok, D., Latham, S., & Rorem, A. (2016). Is kindergarten the new first grade? *Aera Open, 2*(1), 1–31.

Belone, L., Lucero, J. E., Duran, B., Tafoya, G., Baker, E. A., Chan, D., & Wallerstein, N. (2016). Community-based participatory research conceptual model: Community partner consultation and face validity. *Qualitative Health Research, 26,* 117–135.

Benner, A. D., Thornton, A., & Crosnoe, R. (2017). Children's exposure to sustainability practices during the transition from preschool into school and their learning and socioemotional development. *Applied Developmental Science, 21*(2), 121–134.

Bierman, K. L., Domitrovich, C. E., Nix, R. L., Gest, S. D., Welsh, J. A., Greenberg, M. T., & Gill, S. (2008). Promoting academic and social-emotional school readiness: The Head Start REDI program. *Child Development, 79,* 1802–1817.

Blair, C., & Raver, C. C. (2015). School readiness and self-regulation: A developmental psychobiological approach. *Annual Review of Psychology, 66,* 711–731.

Bogard, K., & Takanishi, R. (2005). PK-3: An aligned and coordinated approach to education for children 3 to 8 years old. *SRCD Social Policy Report, 19*(3), 3–23.

Brooks-Gunn, J. (2003). Do you believe in magic? What we can expect from early childhood intervention programs. *SRCD Social Policy Report, 17*(1), 3–14.

Brown, C. P., & Lan, Y. C. (2015). A qualitative metasynthesis of how early educators in international contexts address cultural matters that contrast with developmentally appropriate practices. *Early Education and Development, 26,* 22–45.

Bryk, A., & Schneider, B. (2003). *Trust in schools: A core resource for improvement.* New York, NY: Russell Sage.

Burchinal, M., Vandergrift, N., Pianta, R., & Mashburn, A. (2010). Threshold analysis of association between child care quality and child outcomes for low-income children in pre-kindergarten programs. *Early Childhood Research Quarterly, 25,* 166–176.

Calderón, M., Slavin, R., & Sánchez, M. (2011). Effective instruction for English learners. *Future of Children, 21,* 103–127.

Calzada, E. J., Fernandez, Y., & Cortes, D. E. (2010). Incorporating the cultural value of *respeto* into a framework of Latino parenting. *Cultural Diversity and Ethnic Minority Psychology, 16,* 77–86.

Calzada, E. J., Huang, K. Y., Hernandez, M., Soriano, E., Acra, C. F., Dawson-McClure, S., & Brotman, L. (2015). Family and teacher characteristics as predictors of parent involvement in education during early childhood among Afro-Caribbean and Latino immigrant families. *Urban Education, 50,* 870–896.

Campaign for Quality Early Education Coalition. (2013). Rejoinder to Teachstone's "Dual language learners and the CLASS measure." https://www.buildinitiative.org/portals/0/uploads/documents/resource-center/response%20to%20teachstone%20white%20paper_final_june2013.pdf.

Cascio, E. U., & Schanzenbach, D. W. (2013). *The impacts of expanding access to high-quality preschool education* (No. w19735). Washington, DC: National Bureau of Economic Research.

Center for Public Policy Priorities. (2016). *State of Texas children 2016: Race and equity.* Austin, TX: Author.

Chang, F., Crawford, G., Early, D., Bryant, D., Howes, C., Burchinal, M., Barbarin, O., Clifford, R., & Pianta, R. (2007). Spanish-speaking children's social and language development in pre-kindergarten classrooms. *Early Education and Development, 18*, 243-269.

Charmaz, K. (2006). *Constructing grounded theory: A practical guide through qualitative analysis.* Thousand Oaks, CA: Sage.

Cheadle, J. E. (2008). Educational investment, family context, and children's math and reading growth from kindergarten through third grade. *Sociology of Education, 81*, 1-31.

Chira, S. (1992, June 29). Shaking the schools: When Perot took on Texas. *New York Times.*

Cho, S., & Reich, A. (2008). New immigrants, new challenges: High school social studies teachers and English language learner instruction. *Social Studies, 99*, 235-242.

Christenson, S. L., & Sheridan, S. M. (2001). *School and families: Creating essential connections for learning.* New York, NY: Guilford.

Clarke-Stewart, A., & Allhusen, V. D. (2005). *What we know about childcare.* Cambridge, MA: Harvard University Press.

Clifford, R. M., Barbarin, O., Chang, F., Early, D., Bryant, D., Howes, C., & Pianta, R. (2005). What is pre-kindergarten? Characteristics of public pre-kindergarten programs. *Applied Developmental Science, 9*, 126-143.

Collier, K. (2016, August 16). GOP senators spar over value of pre-K spending. *Texas Tribune.* https://www.texastribune.org/2016/08/16/republican-senators-debate-benefits-pre-k/.

Cooper, C. E., Crosnoe, R., Suizzo, M. A., & Pituch, K. A. (2010). Poverty, race, and parental involvement during the transition to elementary school. *Journal of Family Issues, 31*, 859-883.

Cox, M., & Paley, B. (1997). Families as systems. *Annual Review of Psychology, 48*, 243-267.

Crosnoe, R. (2005). Double disadvantage or signs of resilience: The elementary school contexts of children from Mexican immigrant families. *American Educational Research Journal, 42*, 269-303.

Crosnoe, R. (2006). *Mexican roots, American schools.* Palo Alto, CA: Stanford.

Crosnoe, R. (2010). *Two generation strategies and involving immigrant parents in children's education.* Washington, DC: Urban Institute.

Crosnoe, R. (2012). Family-school connections, early learning, and socioeconomic inequality in the U.S. *Multidisciplinary Journal of Educational Research, 1*, 1-36.

Crosnoe, R. (2015). Continuities and consistencies across home and school systems. In Sheridan, S. M., & Moorman Kim, E. (Eds.), *Research on family-school partnerships: An interdisciplinary examination of the state of the science and critical needs,* volume 2: *Processes and Pathways of Family-School Partnerships* (pp. 61-80). New York: Springer.

Crosnoe, R., & Ansari, A. (2015). Latin American immigrant parents and their children's teachers in US early childhood education programmes. *International Journal of Psychology, 50*, 431-439.

Crosnoe, R., Bonazzo, C., & Wu, N. (2015). *Healthy learners: A whole child approach to disparities in early education.* New York, NY: Teachers College Press.

Crosnoe, R., Leventhal, T., Wirth, R. J., Pierce, K. M., & Pianta, R. C. (2010). Family socioeconomic status and consistent environmental stimulation in early childhood. *Child Development, 81*, 972–987.

Crosnoe, R., & Lopez-Turley, R. (2011). The K-12 educational outcomes of immigrant youth. *Future of Children, 21*, 129–152.

Darling-Hammond, L. (2006). No Child Left Behind and high school reform. *Harvard Educational Review, 76*, 642–667.

de Cohen, C. C., & Clewell, B. C. (2007). *Putting English language learners on the educational map.* Washington, DC: Urban Institute.

Domina, T. (2005). Leveling the home advantage: Assessing the effectiveness of parental involvement. *Sociology of Education, 78*, 233–249.

Domínguez, X., Vitiello, V. E., Fuccillo, J. M., Greenfield, D. B., & Bulotsky-Shearer, R. J. (2011). The role of context in preschool learning: A multilevel examination of the contribution of context-specific problem behaviors and classroom process quality to low-income children's approaches to learning. *Journal of School Psychology, 49*(2), 175–195.

Downer, J. T., López, M. L., Grimm, K. J., Hamagami, A., Pianta, R. C., & Howes, C. (2012). Observations of teacher–child interactions in classrooms serving Latinos and dual language learners: Applicability of the Classroom Assessment Scoring System in diverse settings. *Early Childhood Research Quarterly, 27*(1), 21–32.

Duncan, G. J., & Magnuson, K. (2013). Investing in preschool programs. *Journal of Economic Perspectives, 27*, 109–32.

Dweck, C. S. (2008). *Mindset: The new psychology of success.* New York, NY: Random House.

Eaton, W. (1981). Demographic and social ecologic risk factors for mental disorders. In Regier, D., & Gordon, A. (Eds.), *Risk factor research in the major mental disorders* (pp. 111–130). Washington, DC: US Government Printing Office.

Echevarría, J., Short, D., & Powers, K. (2006). School reform and standards-based education: A model for English language learners. *Journal of Educational Research, 99*, 195–210.

Epstein, J. L. (2005). Attainable goals? The spirit and letter of the No Child Left Behind Act on parental involvement. *Sociology of Education, 78*, 179–182.

Epstein, J. L. (2018). *School, family, and community partnerships: Preparing educators and improving schools.* New York, NY: Routledge.

Flores, A. (2017). *How the U.S. Hispanic population is changing.* Washington, DC: Pew Research Center.

Fry, R. (2011). The Hispanic diaspora and the public schools: Educating Hispanics. In Leal, D., & Trejo, S. (Eds.), *Latinos and the economy* (pp. 15–36). New York: Springer.

Fuller, B. (2007). *Standardized childhood: The political and cultural struggle over early education.* Palo Alto, CA: Stanford University Press.

Fuller, B., Bein, E., Bridges, M., Kim, Y., & Rabe-Hesketh, S. (2017). Do academic preschools yield stronger benefits? Cognitive emphasis, dosage, and early learning. *Journal of Applied Developmental Psychology, 52*, 1–11.

Galindo, C., & Sheldon, S. B. (2012). School and home connections and children's kindergarten achievement gains: The mediating role of family involvement. *Early Childhood Research Quarterly, 27*, 90–103.

Gamoran, A. (2007). *Standards-based reform and the poverty gap: Lessons for No Child Left Behind.* Washington, DC: Brookings Institution Press.

Gamoran, A., Turley, R. N. L., Turner, A., & Fish, R. (2012). Differences between Hispanic and non-Hispanic families in social capital and child development: First-year findings from an experimental study. *Research in Social Stratification and Mobility, 30,* 97–112.

Gándara, P., Maxwell-Jolly, J., & Driscoll, A. (2005). *Listening to teachers of English language learners: A survey of California teachers' challenges, experiences, and professional development needs.* Santa Cruz, CA: University of California Linguistic Minority Research Institute.

Garcia Coll, C., Akiba, D., Palacios, N., Bailey, B., Silver, R., DiMartino, L., & Chin, C. (2002). Parental involvement in children's education: Lessons from three immigrant groups. *Parenting: Science and Practice, 2,* 303–324.

Gathercole, S. E., & Baddeley, A. D. (2014). *Working memory and language processing.* New York, NY: Psychology Press.

Genesee, F., Lindholm-Leary, K., Christian, D., & Saunders, B. (2006). *Educating English language learners: A synthesis of research evidence.* New York, NY: Cambridge University Press.

Genishi, C., & Dyson, A. H. (2009). *Children, language, and literacy: Diverse learners in diverse times.* New York, NY: Teachers College Press.

Ginsburg, M., Block, P H., & McWayne, C. (2010). Partnering to foster achievement in reading and mathematics. In Christenson, S. L., & Reschly, A. L. (Eds.), *Handbook of school-family partnerships* (pp. 193–221). New York, NY: Routledge.

Goldenberg, C. (2008). Teaching English language learners: What the research does—and does not—say. *American Educator, 32,* 8–23.

Goldenberg, L., & Light, D. (2009). *Lee y Seras: Evaluation report.* New York, NY: Education Development Center.

Gormley, W., Gayer, T., Phillips, D., & Dawson, B. (2005). The effects of universal pre-K on cognitive development. *Developmental Psychology, 41,* 872–884.

Grant, K. B., & Ray, J. A. (Eds.). (2018). *Home, school, and community collaboration: Culturally responsive family engagement.* Los Angeles, CA: Sage.

Graue, E. (2008). Teaching and learning in a post-DAP world. *Early Education and Development, 19*(3), 441–447.

Hamilton, R. (2010, March 11). The Texas of today is the U.S. of tomorrow. *Texas Tribune.* https://www.texastribune.org/2010/03/11/former-census-director-talks-demographic-shift/.

Hamre, B. K., Justice, L., Pianta, R., Kilday, C., Sweeney, B., Downer, J., & Leach, A. (2010). Implementation fidelity of MyTeachingPartner literacy and language activities: Association with preschoolers' language and literacy growth. *Early Childhood Research Quarterly, 25,* 329–347.

Harwood, R. L., Schoelmerich, A., Schulze, P. A., & Gonzalez, Z. (1999). Cultural differences in maternal beliefs and behaviors: A study of middle-class Anglo and Puerto Rican mother-infant pairs in four everyday situations. *Child Development, 70,* 1005–1016.

Heckman, J. (2006). Skill formation and the economics of investing in disadvantaged children. *Science, 312,* 1900–1902.

Hemphill, F. C., Vanneman, A., & Rahman, T. (2011). *Achievement gaps: How His-*

panic and white students in public schools perform in mathematics and reading on the National Assessment of Educational Progress (Statistical Analysis Report NCES 2011-459). Washington, DC: National Center for Education Statistics.

Hernandez, D. (2006). *Young Hispanic children in the U.S.: A demographic portrait based on Census 2000: A report to the National Task Force on Early Childhood Education for Hispanics*. Tempe, AZ: National Task Force on Early Childhood Education for Hispanics.

Hernandez, D. J., Denton, N. A., & Macartney, S. E. (2007). Young Hispanic children in the 21st century. *Journal of Latinos and Education, 6*, 209–228.

Hill, N. E. (2001). Parenting and academic socialization as they relate to school readiness: The roles of ethnicity and family income. *Journal of Educational Psychology, 93*(4), 686–697.

Hill, N. E., & Tyson, D. F. (2009). Parental involvement in middle school: A meta-analytic assessment of the strategies that promote achievement. *Developmental Psychology, 45*, 740–763.

Hoover-Dempsey, K. V., & Sandler, H. M. (1997). Why do parents become involved in their children's education? *Review of Educational Research, 67*(1), 3–42.

Hopper, K. (2012). *Preparing young Latino children for school success: Best practices in professional development*. Washington, DC: National Council of La Raza.

Howes, C., Burchinal, M., Pianta, R., Bryant, D., Early, D., Clifford, R., & Barbarin, O. (2008). Ready to learn? Children's pre-academic achievement in prekindergarten programs. *Early Childhood Research Quarterly, 23*, 27–50.

Ivankova, N. V., Creswell, J. W., & Stick, S. L. (2006). Using mixed-methods sequential explanatory design: From theory to practice. *Field Methods, 18*, 3–20.

Jensen, B., Whiting, E. F., & Chapman, S. (2018). Measuring the multicultural dispositions of preservice teachers. *Journal of Psychoeducational Assessment, 36*, 120–135.

Justice, L. M., Mashburn, A., Hamre, B. K., & Pianta, R. (2008). Quality of language and literacy instruction in preschool classrooms serving at-risk pupils. *Early Childhood Research Quarterly, 23*, 51–68.

Karabenick, S. A., & Noda, P. A. C. (2004). Professional development implications of teachers' beliefs and attitudes toward English language learners. *Bilingual Research Journal, 28*, 55–75.

Karoly, L., & Gonzalez, G. (2011). Early care and education for children in immigrant families. *Future of Children, 21*, 71–101.

Kauerz, K. (2006). *Ladders of learning: Fighting fadeout by advancing PK3 alignment*. Washington, DC: New America Foundation.

Kauerz, K., & Coffman, J. (2012). *Evaluating preK-3rd grade reforms*. New York: Foundation for Child Development.

Kemmis, S., & McTaggart, R. (2005). Participatory action research: Communicative action and the public sphere. In Denzin, N. K., & Lincoln, Y. S. (Eds.), *The Sage handbook of qualitative research* (pp. 559–603). Thousand Oaks, CA: Sage.

Krogstad, J. M. (2016). *Five facts about Latinos and education*. Washington, DC: Pew Research Center.

Landry, S. H., Anthony, J. L., Swank, P. R., & Monseque-Bailey, P. (2009). Effectiveness of comprehensive professional development for teachers of at-risk preschoolers. *Journal of Educational Psychology, 101*(2), 448–465.

Landry, S. H., Swank, P. R., Anthony, J. L., & Assel, M. A. (2011). An experimental study evaluating professional development activities within a state funded pre-kindergarten program. *Reading and Writing, 24,* 971-1010.

Lareau, A. (2003). *Unequal childhoods: Class, race, and family life.* Berkeley, CA: University of California Press.

Lauen, D., & Gaddis, S. M. (2012). Shining a light or fumbling in the dark? The effects of NCLB's subgroup-specific accountability on student achievement. *Educational Evaluation and Policy Analysis, 34,* 185-208.

Le, V. N., Schaack, D., Neishi, K., Hernandez, M. W., & Blank, R. (2019). Advanced content coverage at kindergarten: Are there trade-offs between academic achievement and social-emotional skills? *American Educational Research Journal, 56*(4), 1254-1280.

Lee, V. E., & Burkham, D. (2002). *Inequality at the starting gate: Social background differences in achievement as children begin school.* Washington, DC: Economic Policy Institute.

Lerner, R. M. (2006). Developmental science, developmental systems, and contemporary theories of human development. In R. M. Lerner (Ed.), *Theoretical models of human development: Handbook of child psychology* (Vol. 1, pp. 1-17). Hoboken, NJ: Wiley.

Lichter, D. T., & Johnson, K. M. (2009). Immigrant gateways and Hispanic migration to new destinations. *International Migration Review, 43,* 496-518.

Li-Grining, C., Raver, C., Champion, K., Sardin, L., Metzger, M., & Jones, S. (2010). Understanding and improving classroom emotional climate and behavior management in the "real world": The role of Head Start teachers' psychosocial stressors. *Early Education and Development, 21,* 65-94.

Loewenberg, A., Lieberman, A., Garza, R., & Silva, E. (2017). *Implications for preK-12 education in Trump's new budget.* Washington, DC: New America Foundation.

Lopez, G. R., Scribner, J. D., & Mahitivanichcha, K. (2001). Redefining parental involvement: Lessons from high-performing migrant-impacted schools. *American Educational Research Journal, 38,* 253-288.

Ludwig, J., & Phillips, D. (2007). The benefits and costs of Head Start. *SRCD Social Policy Reports, 21,* 3-18.

Madrid, E. M. (2011). The Latino achievement gap. *Multicultural Education, 19,* 7-12.

Magnuson, K., Meyers, M., Ruhm, C., & Waldfogel, J. (2004). Inequality in preschool education and school readiness. *American Educational Research Journal, 41,* 115-157.

Markert, J. (2010). The changing face of racial discrimination: Hispanics as the dominant minority in the USA—a new application of power-threat theory. *Critical Sociology, 36,* 307-327.

Massey, D. S. (Ed.). (2008). *New faces in new places: The changing geography of American immigration.* New York: Russell Sage Foundation.

McWayne, C., Campos, R., & Owsianik, M. (2008). A multidimensional, multilevel examination of mother and father involvement among culturally diverse Head Start families. *Journal of School Psychology, 46,* 551-573.

McWayne, C. M., Melzi, G., Schick, A. R., Kennedy, J. L., & Mundt, K. (2013). Defining family engagement among Latino Head Start parents: A mixed-methods measurement development study. *Early Childhood Research Quarterly, 28,* 593-607.

Meisels, S. J. (2007). Accountability in early childhood: No easy answers. In Pianta, R., Cox, M., & Snow, K. (Eds.), *School readiness and the transition to kindergarten in the era of accountability* (pp. 31–47). Baltimore, MD: Brookes.

Mendez, J., & Crosby, D. (2018). Why and how do low-income Hispanic families search for early care and education? Bethesda, MD: National Research Center on Hispanic Children and Families.

Mendez, J., Crosby, D., & Siskind, D. (2018). Access to early care and education for low-income Hispanic children and families: A research synthesis. Bethesda, MD: National Research Center on Hispanic Children and Families.

Mezulis, A. H., Abramson, L. Y., Hyde, J. S., & Hankin, B. L. (2004). Is there a universal positivity bias in attributions? A meta-analytic review of individual, developmental, and cultural differences in the self-serving attributional bias. *Psychological Bulletin, 130,* 711–747.

Miles, M. B., & Huberman, A. M. (1984). *Qualitative data analysis.* Newbury Park, CA: Sage.

Miller, E., & Almon, J. (2009). Crisis in the kindergarten: Why children need to play in school. College Park, MD: Alliance for Childhood.

National Association for the Education of Young Children. (2019). Position statement on developmentally appropriate practice. Washington, DC: Author.

National Center for Education Statistics. (2019). *English language learners in public schools.* Washington, DC. https://nces.ed.gov/programs/coe/indicator_cgf.asp.

National Institute of Early Education Research [NIEER]. (2013). *The state of preschool: Texas.* New Brunswick, NJ: Author.

National Institute of Early Education Research [NIEER]. (2017). *The state of preschool: Texas.* New Brunswick, NJ: Author.

NICHD Early Child Care Research Network. (2002). Child care and children's development prior to school entry: Results from the NICHD Study of Early Child Care. *American Educational Research Journal, 39,* 133–164.

NICHD Early Child Care Research Network. (2005). *Child care and child development.* New York: Guilford Press.

Paredes, E., Hernandez, E., Herrera, A., & Tonyan, H. (2018). Putting the "family" in family child care: The alignment between familismo (familism) and family child care providers' descriptions of their work. *Early Childhood Research Quarterly.*

Pelletier, J., & Corter, C. (2006). Integration, innovation, and evaluation in school-based early childhood services. In Spodek, B., & Saracho, O. (Eds.), *Handbook of research on the education of young children* (pp. 477–496). Mahwah, NJ: Erlbaum.

Pew Research Center. (2014). *Statistical portrait of Hispanics in the United States.* Washington, DC: Author.

Pianta, R. C., Belsky, J., Houts, R., Morrison, F., & the NICHD Early Child Care Research Network (2007). Opportunities to learn in America's elementary classrooms. *Science, 315*(5820), 1795–1796.

Pianta, R., LaParo, K., & Hamre, B. (2007). *Classroom Scoring Assessment System (CLASS).* Baltimore, MD: Brookes.

Pianta, R. C., & Walsh, D. J. (1996). *High-risk children in schools: Constructing sustaining relationships.* New York, NY: Routledge.

Pianta, R. C., Whittaker, J. E., Vitiello, V., Ansari, A., & Ruzek, E. (2018). Class-

room process and practices in public pre-k programs. *Early Education and Development, 29,* 797-813.
Pollock, M. (2009). *Colormute: Race talk dilemmas in an American school.* Princeton, NJ: Princeton University Press.
Pomerantz, E. M., Moorman, E. A., & Litwack, S. D. (2007). The how, whom, and why of parents' involvement in children's academic lives: More is not always better. *Review of Educational Research, 77*(3), 373.
Puma, M., Bell, S., Cook, R., Held, C., Shapiro, G., Broene, P., Jenkins, F., Fletcher, P., Quinn, L., Friedman, J., Ciarico, J., Rohacek, M., Adams, G., & Spier, E. (2010). *Head Start impact study.* Washington, DC: US Department of Health and Human Services.
Ramirez, A. Y. F. (2003). Dismay and disappointment: Parental involvement of Latino immigrant parents. *Urban Review, 35,* 93-110.
Raver, C. (2002). Emotions matter: Making the case for the role of young children's emotional development for early school readiness. *Social Policy Report, 16*(3), 3-19.
Raver, C. C., Gershoff, E. T., & Aber, J. L. (2007). Testing equivalence of mediating models of income, parenting, and school readiness for white, black, and Hispanic children in a national sample. *Child Development, 78*(1), 96-115.
Ream, R. (2003). Counterfeit social capital and Mexican-American underachievement. *Educational Evaluation and Policy Analysis, 25,* 237-262.
Reardon, S., & Galindo, C. (2009). The Hispanic-white achievement gap in math and reading in the elementary school grades. *American Educational Research Journal, 46,* 853-891.
Reardon, S. F., & Owens, A. (2014). 60 years after Brown: Trends and consequences of school segregation. *Annual Review of Sociology, 40,* 199-218.
Reese, L., Balzano, S., Gallimore, R., & Goldenberg, C. (1995). The concept of *educación*: Latino family values and American schooling. *International Journal of Educational Research, 23,* 57-81.
Ressler, R. (2020). What village? Opportunities and supports for parental involvement outside of the family context. *Children and Youth Services Review,* 108.
Reynolds, A. J., & Shlafer, R. J. (2010). Parent involvement in early education. In Christenson, S. L., & Reschly, A. L. (Eds.), *Handbook of school-family partnerships* (pp. 176-192). New York, NY: Routledge.
Rimm-Kaufman, S. E., & Pianta, R. C. (2000). An ecological perspective on the transition to kindergarten: A theoretical framework to guide empirical research. *Journal of Applied Developmental Psychology, 21,* 491-511.
Rivas-Drake, D., & Marchand, A. (2016). Academic socialization among Latino families: Exploring the compensatory role of cultural processes. *Research in Human Development, 13,* 225-240.
Robinson, K., & Harris, A. L. (2014). *The broken compass: Parental involvement with children's education.* Cambridge, MA: Harvard University Press.
Russakoff, D. (2011). *PreK-3rd: Raising the educational performance of English language learners.* New York, NY: Foundation for Child Development.
Ryan, G., & Bernard, H. R. (2003). Techniques to identify themes. *Field Methods, 15,* 85-109.
Ryan, S., & Grieshaber, S. (2005). Shifting from developmental to postmodern practices in early childhood teacher education. *Journal of Teacher Education, 56*(1), 34-45.

Sameroff, A. (1983). Developmental systems: Context and evolution. In P. Mussen (Ed.), *Handbook of Child Psychology* (Vol. 1, pp. 237–294). New York, NY: Wiley.

Schweinhart, L. J., Montie, J., Zongping, X., Barnett, W. S., Belfield, C. R., & Nores, M. (2005). *Lifetime effects: The High/Scope Perry Preschool study through age 40.* Ypsilanti, MI: HighScope.

Severns, M. (2014, August 22). The GOP's new take on pre-K. *Politico.* https://www.politico.com/story/2014/08/22/republicans-pre-kindergarten-1346456.

Sheridan, S. M., & Moorman Kim, E. M. (Eds.). (2015). *Family-school partnerships in context.* New York, NY: Springer.

Solórzano, R. W. (2008). High stakes testing: Issues, implications, and remedies for English language learners. *Review of Educational Research, 78*, 260–329.

Stanton-Salazar, R. D. (2001). *Manufacturing hope and despair: The school and kin support networks of U.S.-Mexican youth.* New York, NY: Teacher's College Press.

Stipek, D., Franke, M., Clements, D., Farran, D., & Coburn, C. (2017). PK-3: What does it mean for instruction? *Society for Research in Child Development Social Policy Report, 30*(2), 1–23.

Suarez-Orozco, C., & Suarez-Orosco, M. (2001). *Children of immigration.* Cambridge, MA: Harvard University Press.

Takanishi, R. (2004). Leveling the playing field: Supporting immigrant children from birth to eight. *Future of Children, 14*, 61–80.

Takanishi, R., & Le Menestrel, S. (Eds.). (2017). *Fostering school success for English learners: Toward new directions in policy, practice, and research.* Washington, DC: National Academies Press.

Texas Demographic Center. (2016). Texas and San Antonio population and children. http://demographics.texas.gov/Resources/Presentations/OSD/2016/2016_09_30_CongressonChildren.pdf.

Texas Early Childhood Education Coalition. (2005). *The Texas plan: A statewide early education and development system* (2nd ed.). www.tecec.org/files/The%20Texas%20Plan,%20Edition%202.pdf.

Texas Education Agency. (2016). *Texas public kindergarten programs and kindergarten readiness.* www.texaseducationinfo.org/Home/Topic/Kindergarten%20Programs%20and%20Readines.

Texas Education Agency. (2017). *Prekindergarten outcomes for Texas public school students.* Austin, TX: Author.

Texas Education Agency. (2018). *High-quality prekindergarten program.* https://tea.texas.gov/Academics/Early_Childhood_Education/High-Quality_Prekindergarten_Program/.

Thomas, W. I., & Thomas, D. S. (1928). *The child in America: Behavior problems and programs.* New York, NY: Knopf.

Tienda, M. (2009). Hispanicity and educational inequality: Risks, opportunities, and the nation's future. American Association of Hispanics in Higher Education Tomas Rivera Lecture. http://www.ets.org/Media/Research/pdf/PICRIVERA1.pdf.

Tobin, J., Adair, J. K., & Arzubiaga, A. (2013). *Children crossing borders: Immigrant parent and teacher perspectives on preschool for children of immigrants.* New York: Russell Sage Foundation.

Turner, K., Guzman, L., Wildsmith, E., & Scott, M. (2015). *The complex and varied households of low-income Hispanic children.* Washington, DC: National Research Center on Hispanic Children and Families.

US Census Bureau. (2018). Quick facts: Texas. https://www.census.gov/quickfacts/tx.

Valdés, G. (1996). *Con respeto: Bridging the distances between culturally diverse families and schools: An ethnographic portrait.* New York, NY: Teachers College Press.

Villenas, S., & Foley, D. (2002). Chicano/Latino critical ethnography of education: Cultural productions from la frontera. In Valencia, R., (Ed.), *Chicano school failure and success* (pp. 195–226). New York, NY: Routledge.

Vitiello, V. E. (2013). *Dual language learners and the CLASS measure: Research and recommendations.* Charlottesville, VA: Teachstone Training.

Waldfogel, J. (2006). *What children need.* Cambridge, MA: Harvard University Press.

Wallerstein, N., & Duran, B. (2010). Community-based participatory research contributions to intervention research: the intersection of science and practice to improve health equity. *American Journal of Public Health, 100,* S40–S46.

Wasik, B. A., & Hindman, A. H. (2011). Improving vocabulary and pre-literacy skills of at-risk preschoolers through teacher professional development. *Journal of Educational Psychology, 103*(2), 455–469.

Weisberg, D. S., Hirsh-Pasek, K., & Golinkoff, R. M. (2013). Guided play: Where curricular goals meet a playful pedagogy. *Mind, Brain, and Education, 7,* 104–112.

White House, Office of the Press Secretary. (2013). *Fact sheet: President Obama's plan for early education for all Americans.* Washington, DC: Author.

Yoshikawa, H., & Hsueh, J. (2001). Child development and public policy: Towards a dynamic systems perspective. *Child Development, 72,* 1887–1903.

Zigler, E., Gilliam, W. S., & Jones, S. M. (2006). *A vision for universal preschool education.* New York: Cambridge University Press.

Index

academic and cognitive development, 2, 6, 65, 68, 89, 92-96, 108, 110, 114, 118, 131-132, 138, 142, 146. *See also* academically scaffolding classrooms; cognitively stimulating instruction
academically scaffolding classrooms, 68, 89, 93, 95-110, 138-140, 142. *See also* academic and cognitive development; cognitively stimulating instruction
academic standards and accountability movement/philosophy, 5-7, 13, 36-38, 88-89, 138
alignment, 33-34, 36, 40-61, 63, 135-136, 140-141, 143-149; horizontal, 43-45, 47-49, 51-53, 55, 57, 59-60, 135-136, 141, 144-145; self-, 59, 139, 148; vertical, 43-45, 47-49, 51, 53-61, 135-136, 140-141, 144-145, 148
a priori themes, 45, 74, 115, 119, 122, 128-129. *See also* compensation; perceived instructional fit; time constraints
assets vs. deficits (and vice versa), 24, 71, 84, 94, 105, 126-127, 139

bellwethers, 9, 93, 151
bidirectional transactions, 29, 67
bien educado, 71-72, 76, 78, 84, 137, 143
bilingual/dual language instruction, 16, 22, 38, 50-51, 53, 80, 82, 101, 119-120, 123-124, 139. *See also* primarily Spanish-speaking classrooms
bilingualism, 111, 139, 152

Classroom Assessment Scoring System (CLASS), 16-19, 22, 25, 37-38, 46-47, 73, 97-102, 105, 120-122, 128-130, 137-139, 150, 154-156. *See also* classroom organization; emotional support; instructional support
classroom organization, 17-18, 46, 98-101, 129-131, 137, 139. *See also* Classroom Assessment Scoring System (CLASS)
cognitively stimulating instruction, 119-122, 130-131, 139. *See also* academic and cognitive development; academically scaffolding classrooms
Cole Pre-K Campus, 15, 20, 34, 46, 48-49, 55-61, 74-75, 81-84, 86, 97, 101-103, 105, 107-108, 110, 123-125, 128, 136, 138, 144-146
college, 8, 10, 148
color muteness, 155
compensation, 115, 118, 129, 139, 142. *See also* a priori themes
connected processes, 32, 36-37, 88, 135, 141, 143, 144. *See also* contextual systems theory

Index

contextual connections, 32–34, 135, 140, 143–144. *See also* contextual systems theory
contextual systems theory, 22, 28–32, 34, 42, 62, 67, 69, 88, 135, 149–150. *See also* connected processes; contextual connections
counterfeit social capital, 112, 119
cultural grounding, 6, 73, 93–94, 109–110
culture, 6, 70–71, 73, 81, 84–85, 89, 94, 125–126, 152

developmentally appropriate practices movement/philosophy, 6–7, 13, 34, 36–37, 38, 88–89, 103, 108, 135, 138
developmental systems theory, 28–29, 32
direct partnerships, 67–68. *See also* family-school-community partnerships
discrimination, 8, 12, 70, 93, 137, 152
diversity, 7–8, 14, 50, 69, 83, 147–148, 151; linguistic, 8, 14, 50, 148; racial/ethnic, 14, 148; socioeconomic, 69, 148
double disadvantage, 131–132
double duty, 131, 140

early child care, 2, 94, 117, 151
Early Childhood Longitudinal Study, 72
educación, 35, 71, 73, 78
educational policy and initiatives, 1–3, 5, 10, 25, 34–38, 45, 60, 62, 65–66, 91–94, 112–113, 133–134, 145; in Texas, 5, 9–11, 15, 93, 113, 133, 135. *See also* No Child Left Behind act/legislation (NCLB)
emergent themes, 45, 74, 115, 116, 122, 129. *See also* literacy challenges; parent-related challenges; socioeconomic challenges
emotional support, 17–18, 46, 97–101, 129–131, 137, 139. *See also* Classroom Assessment Scoring System (CLASS)
English language learners, 3, 10, 13–15, 17, 19, 37–39, 41, 50–51, 53, 61, 70, 94, 111–120, 122, 124–129, 131–132, 139, 142
established immigrant/latina/o destinations, 11–12

fade-out, 4, 6, 10, 33, 41–43, 60
familismo, 71
family-school-community partnerships, 10, 23, 34–36, 62–63, 67–74, 76–80, 83, 85–87, 127, 136–137, 140, 141, 146–149. *See also* direct partnerships; indirect partnerships
federal immigration policy, 7, 134

grounded theory, 44, 115, 150

Head Start, 2–4, 9–10, 16, 134

indirect partnerships, 68. *See also* family-school-community partnerships
instructional demand, 112, 117
instructional support, 17–18, 46, 97–102, 105, 119–122, 129–131, 137–139, 147, 151. *See also* Classroom Assessment Scoring System (CLASS)

latinization of population, 7, 11–12
linguistic barriers, 8, 12, 22–23, 63, 70, 79, 86, 93, 132, 137, 143, 148
literacy challenges, 123–124, 128, 139. *See also* emergent themes

mixed method sequential explanatory design, 155
monolingualism, 111, 152

new immigrant/latina/o destinations, 11–12, 14
No Child Left Behind act/legislation (NCLB), 5, 10, 35, 62. *See also* educational policy and initiatives

parental involvement in education, 3, 56, 58, 63–72, 75, 77, 80, 82–84, 86–87, 127

parent-related challenges, 127–128. *See also* emergent themes
parent-support specialists, 86, 146, 148
perceived instructional fit, 114, 117–118, 124, 128–129, 139. *See also* a priori themes
Perot, H. Ross, 9, 11
PK-3 movement/philosophy, 4, 22, 34, 40–44, 58, 60, 63
poverty, 8, 12–13, 52, 68–69, 75, 80–81, 93, 118, 125–127, 137, 139, 143, 152
primarily Spanish-speaking classrooms, 22, 38, 101, 104, 109, 119–123, 125–130, 138–140, 142. *See also* bilingual/dual language instruction
professional development, 11, 19, 41, 44, 52–56, 59, 61, 86, 116–117, 136, 141, 147
public early childhood education movement, 89–90, 93, 133
public preschool programs, 3, 9–11, 13, 15, 16, 23, 42, 46, 60, 98, 113, 134, 141

respeto, 34, 71–72, 76, 78, 84, 137

school readiness, 10–11, 13, 15, 17, 38, 45, 86, 91–93, 107, 123, 129, 131–132
Sheltered Instruction Observation Protocol, 120
socioeconomic challenges, 125–127, 139. *See also* emergent themes
socioemotional development, 6, 37–38, 68, 88–89, 92–95, 106–109, 112, 118, 129, 131, 138, 142, 147. *See also* socioemotionally supportive classrooms
socioemotionally supportive classrooms, 68, 89, 93–110, 138–140, 142. *See also* socioemotional development
standardized testing, 4–5, 10, 13, 15, 57, 113, 116, 151
stratification, 8, 63, 69, 73, 93, 148; racial/ethnic, 69; socioeconomic, 8, 148

time constraints, 115–116, 128, 142, 147. *See also* a priori themes

"whole child," the, 6, 10, 89, 95, 97, 102, 108